Is It Possible to Live This Way?

Volume 3: Charity

Is It Possible to Live This Way?

An Unusual Approach to Christian Existence

Volume 3: Charity

LUIGI GIUSSANI

McGill-Queen's University Press
Montreal & Kingston | London | Chicago

© McGill-Queen's University Press 2009
ISBN 978-0-7735-3514-5 (cloth)
ISBN 978-0-7735-3515-2 (paper)
ISBN 978-0-7735-7532-5 (ePDF)
ISBN 978-0-7735-8159-3 (ePUB)

Reprinted 2020

Legal deposit third quarter 2009
Bibliothèque nationale du Québec

Printed in Canada on acid-free paper that is 100% ancient forest free
(100% post-consumer recycled), processed chlorine free

Library and Archives Canada Cataloguing in Publication
Giussani, Luigi
    Is it possible to live this way?: an unusual approach
    to Christian existence / Luigi Guissani.

    Translation of Si può vivere così?
    Includes bibliographical references.
    Contents: v. 1. Faith - v. 2. Hope. - v. 3. Charity.
    ISBN 978-0-7735-3403-2 (v. 1: bound). – ISBN 978-0-7735-3404-9
    (v. 1: pbk.). – ISBN 978-0-7735-7470-0 (v. 1: ePDF). – ISBN 978-0-
    7735-7776-3 (v. 1: ePUB). – ISBN 978-0-7735-3445-2 (v. 2: bound). –
    ISBN 978-0-7735-3446-9 (v. 2: pbk.). – ISBN 978-0-7735-7471-7
    (v. 2: ePDF). – ISBN 978-0-7735-7777-0 (v. 2: ePUB). –
    ISBN 978-0-7735-3514-5 (v. 3: bound). – ISBN 978-0-7735-3515-2
    (v. 3: pbk.). – ISBN 978-0-7735-7532-5 (v. 3: ePDF). –
    ISBN 978-0-7735-8159-3 (v. 3: ePUB).

    1. Spiritual life – Catholic Church. 2. Christian youth – Religious life.
    1. Title.
    BX2350.3.G4813 2008   234'.23   C2008-900458-2

Typeset in Bembo with Futura 11/15
by Infoscan Collette, Quebec City

Contents

Note on the Translation

This work was translated piecemeal over a number of years, primarily by Dino Gerard D'Agata, Barbara Gagliotti, and Chris Vath. It was subsequently edited by Damian Bacich and John Zucchi and proofread by John Kinder. Lesley Andrassy copy-edited the final manuscript. I have tried to keep the edition as free as possible of editorial notes, but it is useful to point out a few recurring names and an acronym. *Memores Domini* refers to a "private universal ecclesial association" (a juridical designation in Canon Law). Members are lay men and women who dedicate their lives to God. They are also traditionnally known as the *Gruppo Adulto* (Adult Group). Communion and Liberation (CL) is a lay movement in the Catholic Church. The author, Luigi Giussani, founded it in 1954, while he was a high school teacher. Originally he called it GS, which stands for *Gioventù Studentesca* (Student Youth). He often refers to CL in the text as "the Movement." For a brief overview of Giussani and his work, the reader might consult John Zucchi, "Luigi Giussani, the Church, and Youth in the 1950s: A Judgment Born of an Experience," in *Logos* 10:4, 131–50, or www.clonline.org.

John Zucchi
General Editor, English language edition

By Way of Introduction

This is an unusual book. It is a kind of "novel," as those who first read the proofs noted. In this work the discovery of life as "vocation" comes about not through deduction but through the evidence of an experience lived according to reason, within the same breath as Mystery. It deals with the path that Father Luigi Giussani took throughout a year in dialogue with about one hundred young people who had decided to commit their lives to Christ through total dedication to the Mystery and to His destiny in history. The Church calls this life "virginity." Week after week the principal contents of the Christian faith and the reasons that sustained them were approached through a proposal that emerged from the author's experience and from the passionate dynamic of questions and answers that was awakened in these young people. Thus they gradually became aware of their human experience and lived it in a more determined way.

The style of these weekly meetings has been faithfully maintained in the book as a testimony to a particular approach to the great human problem and to the mature conviction and affection that it can lead to.

The book is not meant to be a challenge to common sense or to be presumptuous. It began as a faithful transcription of meetings and dialogues. It is thus a test or, better yet, a witness to a way of conceiving of Christian faith as something interesting, as a destiny for life. It is transcribed word for word, in its material immediacy. In that sense the repetition of ideas and formulae is aimed at filling one's memory in such a way that it might retain something that will be understood over the years and whose reasons will gradually be grasped.

The book can be conceived of as an exemplary narrative where spontaneity, loyalty, and seriousness in the consideration of one's own existence are able to ascribe a suggestiveness to something that most people would censure or disdain because of an abstract fear.

Is It Possible to Live This Way?

Volume 3: Charity

1 Charity

Today let's talk about the third column that holds the temple of God in place: reality as the temple of God, reality as it is lived by man, because it is the temple of God to the degree that it is lived by man. Earlier, during morning prayer, we sang: "the earth echoes forth hymns of gladness to Christ who has risen from death."[1]; It is in our awareness that the earth echoes forth hymns of gladness. The earth does not move, the earth does not laugh, the earth is not joyful; neither is a dog, even if it has its eyes wide open, with a kind of smile in them, filled with who knows what sensation (as Miguel Mañara says when, because of Girolama's influence, he reawakens; it's as if he reawakened after a long illness. Do you remember that passage from *Miguel Mañara*?[2]). Man is not a dog; for this reason, the earth echoes forth hymns of gladness through the awareness of man. Man's awareness is his capacity to order all things towards their destiny, towards their origin and their destiny: this awareness unites things, and thus it is the Creator's tool for completing His work.

1 THE INTIMACY OF A PRESENCE
THAT FAITH RECOGNIZES

Charity, this third column that holds up the great temple of God that is the world, indicates the deepest content, discovers intimacy, discovers the heart of that Presence that faith recognizes.

There's a chapter in the gospel that, after you've read it fifty-four times, will sink in a little, because it is synthesizes what we'd like to begin with: the seventeenth chapter of Saint John, the testament of Jesus.

Let's start taking the steps necessary to understand something, slowly. Then you can go over them at home, although these things penetrate us as through osmosis, through osmotic pressure, rather than through a banal analysis that claims to clarify things. They enter into us if we look at the mystery of Christ, like John and Andrew, who watched Him speak without interrupting Him.

Charity indicates the deepest and most intimate content of that supreme reality that faith allows us to recognize. Faith is obliged to make us recognize it. Why are we obliged to recognize it? To be obliged means we would not be reasonable if we didn't recognize it. Why? Because reason is awareness of reality according to the totality of its factors. We are in front of a factor that corresponds to the needs of our heart – or better yet, it brings those needs out, as in the case of one who stands on tiptoes to see something he wants to see yet still doesn't see it; he stretches his neck and still doesn't see it, but the thing is there, because its voice is heard. This factor is inexplicable; that is, you can't deduce it through human experience.

The most intimate content of the supreme reality exists in experience, because it is felt, and, when followed, it produces an effect, it changes things. But above all, it dialogues imperiously with the heart and answers one, another, and yet another need: the constitutive needs of our spirit. We can understand neither how nor when, but His exceptional physiognomy, His exceptional Presence, is there. If I don't recognize Him as present because I don't understand it, because I don't understand how He can be present, I go against reason, because reason says either "He exists" or "He doesn't exist." To say "He exists," while adding "I don't know how to explain it," leaves reason perfectly and honorably in accord with itself. In addition, from the moment of the encounter, what reason desires to be able to understand most (to be able to enter into, to be able to walk inside of!) is that thing there. But it understands that it can't even show how this can happen; it must simply follow what appeared in its present experience – unthinkable, unforeseeable, not a consequence of prior factors (as it says in "The Journeying").[3]

Without "reasons"

Before explaining the two factors that must be clarified to begin to understand the word "charity," it would be useful to remember that the word's etymology is already meaningful. Charity comes from the Greek *caris*, which means free or gratuitous. Charity, then, recalls the highest form of the expression of love. Gratuitousness – from which every calculation is banished, every expectation of recompense, every expectation of self-interest – implies the total absence of "reasons" comprehended by reason, explained by reason. Charity implies the absence of reasons, that is, the absence of self-interest, of calculation, of a proportionality regarding an expectation; in other words, the absence of something in return. The reason for an action is what the action provides in return. It is a recompense: for carrying out that action, I am paid on the twenty-seventh of the month. For giving money to this person, for giving gifts to that person, I get something in return: his or her attachment to me, which I feel a need for as affection or which I feel as a need for collaboration in something. Listen, charity totally abolishes – totally, in the absolute sense of the term – every recompense. That means that charity acts out of pure love, only out of love.

Only out of love? Even someone who gives money to another while calculating the return acts out of love. Charity acts out of pure love in the sense that it's given, it's done. Given, done; there's nothing added, there is no appendage.

That person doesn't acknowledge me? It doesn't matter, I do it just the same. And what is love if not wanting the good of another? Not wanting something for me, but wanting the good of another – the good of another is his relationship with his destiny. The relationship with his destiny is the relationship with a Presence, because his destiny became Someone who walks along the streets, takes children in His arms, who looks at society and weeps from atop the hill, who was taken for a criminal – and the assassin was freed while He was crucified.

Charity is pure love, so it is said. It is fulfilled in wanting the good of another; this good is the good that one desires for the other. It is his destiny, it is his relationship with Christ.

Some of these steps may be implicit in those who live charity, without their being aware of them.

The reason for charity

Even charity is sustained by a reason; if it weren't, it would be unreasonable. Charity is a gesture that is human, and if it weren't sustained by a reason, it would be unreasonable. But the reason that sustains charity is totally and exclusively the object of love, the authentic object of love. What is the authentic object of love? It is the good of another, the destiny of another, therefore his relationship with Christ. The only reason for charity – that is, for gratuitousness – is this, the most human reason that exists, because even animals can make calculations.

2 CHARITY: THE GIFT OF THE SELF, MOVED

Since this is the theme that must dominate our lives, I said that today we would take the first steps, which you will then develop in your weekly meetings, your group conversations or your personal meditation, but above all in your begging attitude towards Christ – you will live towards Christ.

Two things make up the Christian characteristic of charity. Charity is a word everyone can use: "Do it for me out of charity, Mr Deputy: give me this post on the advisory board. Do it out of charity!" We, instead, will speak today of the authentic and Christian concept of charity; that is, of the true concept of love. Why is charity the true concept of love? Because the reason for it is the exhaustive reason, the only one, the exhaustive one, of love: the reason of love that identifies the object it desires with the other's good, the other's destiny. How can we succeed in understanding the figure of Christ or read a page of the gospel with intelligence and the necessary emotion if we don't keep this in mind? Why did Jesus look around Him? Excuse me, why is Carlo interested in you? I remember that day when he came to tell me that his professor would give him the Chair of Chemistry at the University of Palermo. And he said: "I am going to refuse it, because if I accept it, I will lose my vocation." What was his vocation if not that which you see him doing? For whom? For you. And who are you? Who makes him do it?

a) A pure gift of self

First, God's relationship with man, the Mystery's relationship with man – let's say the Mystery, because Mystery is God and Christ, it is God and man – the Mystery appears to man as gratuitousness; that is, as charity. You can even say what Saint John said: God's very nature is charity.[4] Nature is that factor by which one acts in a certain way; nature is the origin of actions; therefore, if one acts with charity, it is because one has the nature that is the origin of charity. And he says: "Deus caritas est," God is love, but love in its total, absolute sense: it wants the other's good.

God's nature appears as gratuitousness insofar as it has been given to man. Gift: this is the first word the term "gratuitousness," or the term "charity," or the term "love" attaches itself to. It is a pure gift, we said: without something in return. Without something in return means that it is a pure gift. God's nature is to give; He appears to man as giving, as a gift, without something in return, a pure gift.

What does He give you? Himself, which is to say, Being; Being, because without Him nothing of what was made would have been made. "Without me you can do nothing."[5] Imagine that scene, the night of Holy Thursday. Everything was against them, and Jesus spoke, spoke – that long discourse we read together on Holy Thursday.[6] Those men who were accustomed to hearing Him speak stared at Him while He spoke, observing all His actions; they were more attentive to Him than usual; everyone was attentive. That man who had put His hand in the dish to eat together with them – as they did back then – at a certain point interrupts and says: "Without me you can do nothing." This is God, the only one who can say this is God!

God's nature appears to man as an absolute gift: God gives Himself, gives His very self to man. And what is God? The source of being. God gives man being: He gives man the ability to be; He gives man the ability to be greater, to grow; He gives man the ability to be completely himself, to grow to fulfillment; that is, He gives man the ability to be happy (happy – that is, totally satisfied or perfect. As I've always said, in Latin and in Greek, "perfect" and "satisfied" are the same word: *perfectus*, that is, perfect or fulfilled. A man who is fulfilled is a man who is satisfied).

He gave Himself to me by giving me His being: "Let us make man in our own image and likeness."[7] And then, when man least expected it – he couldn't even dream about it, he no longer expected it, he no longer thought about Him from whom he had received being – this "Him" re-enters man's life to save it, He gives Himself again, dying for man. He gives everything, a total gift of self, until: "There is no greater love than to lay down one's life for one's friends."[8] A total gift.

But here, there is a final nuance. What Christ gives us in dying for us – dying because we betrayed Him – so as to purify us from the betrayal, is greater than what was owed to us. This is like an angle opened on the infinite, to be considered as you go through your life, something to be experienced. Christ gives us more than what was necessary to save us: where sin abounds, gratuitousness overabounds. He did more than what was necessary to save us. To save us, Christ could have merely said: "Father, forgive them"; that was enough. While He reclined to eat the last supper, He could have said: "Father, forgive them." That would have been enough. It would even have been enough for Him to say: "Yes, Father, send me," and enter into Mary's womb, becoming a baby, becoming a man. This alone would have been enough. But no: "Where sin abounded, grace overflowed all the more."[9] However, the fundamental concept that explains the entire value of the term charity or gratuitousness – which delineates God's nature, God's way of acting, which we must imitate because

He is the Father – is the gift of self. Morality is the gift of self, as the eighth chapter in the second book of the School of Community explains.[10] Not only that, but it forgives man's betrayal, man's disregard, his denial ...

To understand what betrayal is, my friends, we have to think of our own distraction, because it is a betrayal to spend days, weeks, months ... what about last night, when did we think of Him? When did we seriously think of Him, with our heart, in this last month, in the last three months, from October until now? Never. We haven't thought of Him as John and Andrew thought of Him while they watched Him speak. If we asked a lot of questions about Him, it was out of curiosity, analysis, the need for analysis, for research, for clarification, for clarification. But we need to think the way one who is really in love thinks about his beloved (even in this case it happens extremely rarely because everything is calculated to get something in return!); solely in a way that is absolutely, totally detached – a sole desire for the good ... so much so that if the other doesn't respond in kind, the desire for the other's good is nourished even more!

b) Moved

The second factor – the first is the essential one – is like an adjective next to a noun, it's descriptive. Adjective means that it rests, it rests on the noun, therefore it would be secondary to the first. Nevertheless, it is the most impressive, and we – I am willing to bet you – have never thought of it and would never think of it, if God had not put us together.

Why does God dedicate Himself to me? Why does He give Himself to me, in creating me, giving me being, that is, Himself (He gives me Himself, that is, being)? Moreover, why does He become man and give Himself to me to make me innocent once again – as today's hymn says[11] – and die for me (which there was absolutely no need for: a snap of the fingers and the Father would have certainly done it)? Why does He die for me? Why this gift of self up to the conceivable extreme, beyond the conceivable extreme?

Here you must go to see and learn the sentence of the prophet Jeremiah by heart, in the thirty-first chapter, from verse 3 onward. Through the voice of the prophet that is fulfilled in Christ (think of the people who were there together with that man, that young man who fulfilled these things), God says: "With eternal love I have loved you, for this I have attracted you to me [that is, I let you share in my nature], having pity on your nothingness." I have always translated this sentence in this way. What does "having pity on your nothingness" mean? What is it about? A feeling, a feeling! It is about a value that is a feeling, because affection is a feeling. To have "affection for" is a feeling, yet it is a value. To the degree that it has reason, it is a value; if it is does not have reason, no type of affection is a value because it is missing half of the I, the I is truncated: only what is below the navel remains.

It is beautiful to come across this pity – "having pity on your nothingness" – in the gospel. For example, when – it is said twice – Jesus sees his city from the hill one night and cries over it, thinking of its ruin.[12] Weeks later that city would kill Him, but for Him this doesn't matter.

Or that other night, immediately before He was taken, in the golden splendour of the temple illuminated by the setting sun, *edakruse*, the Greek text says, "He sobbed," in front of his city's destiny.[13] It is pity like that of a mother who clings to her child so he does not fall into the mortal danger he's headed for.

And then, I'll choose from Saint Luke first, because in Saint Luke this is more noticeable than in any other gospel (Saint Luke with Saint John and Saint Mark and Saint Matthew; Saint Matthew was a Jew, Saint Luke was a pagan): He's walking through the countryside with his disciples and they're breaking off ears of wheat, because they were hungry. They see a funeral passing by in the nearby town. He asks: "What is it?" "It's a young guy – *adulescens*, an adolescent – who died and his mother is a widow. She lost her only son and she is a widow." In fact the mother is wailing behind the coffin. Jesus walks over and says: "Woman, don't cry," which was something inconceivable. Aside from the fact that it's between the ridiculous and the absurd, how can you tell a woman in that condition, who follows her son's coffin, "Don't cry"? It was the overflowing of pity, of compassion.[14]

Or we can imagine when He passes under that tree in which Zaccheus is crouching above him: Zaccheus, the Mafia boss of the entire northeastern part of Jerusalem, of Jericho. He stops. The last thought Zaccheus had was this. He stops and looks at him: "Zaccheus [he says his name],

Zaccheus, come down quickly, for today I'm going to your house."[15] There isn't any possibility of this kind of tenderness among us; we are gruesome, boorish, we are stones compared to this situation here: "Zaccheus."

Or (and these are the more symptomatic cases) when He learned that his friend Lazarus was dead: "And He wept." He was three days away – a long trip to take. As soon as He heard, He wept. So much so that the Jews who were there near Him said afterward: "Could not the one who opened the eyes of the man born blind have done something about the death of His friend?"[16] Think of what bonds of affection there must have been.

What I want to say is that God's charity for man – this gift of self – is made up of an emotion, of being moved. You can have compassion for a stricken animal that's dying, but you can't be moved by it. For man, you can.

God's charity for man is being moved, a gift of self that vibrates, agitates, moves, is fulfilled in emotion, in the reality of being moved: it is moved. God who is moved! "What is man that you should be mindful of him?" says the psalm.[17]

There is a passage in the gospel that isn't very well known – I had it read during Holy Week for the first time. It's the twelfth chapter of Saint John. When He was about to be taken – He knew that on that night they would take Him, yet He was still in the midst of the people – there in Jerusalem, for the Passover, in the temple, was a group of pagans who went there out of curiosity. "Now there were some Greek pagans among those who had come up to worship at the feast. They came to Philip, who was from

Bethsaida in Galilee (from the historical point of view this has enormous value – as you should know if you read the articles in *Il Sabato* and *30 Days*,[18] or more importantly, the historical and exegetical books written on the evangelical texts and their origin – because Bethsaida was a point of convergence for caravans from the entire geographical horizon, which means that in Bethsaida everyone knew Greek – but in the Gospel this is taken for granted, nothing has to be explained to anyone). They came to Philip, who was from Bethsaida in Galilee, and asked him, "Sir, [even the word they used was a word of respect in the pagan, Greek, vocabulary] we would like to see Jesus [we want to see Jesus. Who is this Jesus?]." Philip went and told Andrew (another one who didn't know what to do); then Andrew and Phillip went and told Jesus. Jesus answered them, "The hour has come for the Son of Man to be glorified [the first time that what He came for, the entire world, the pagan reality of the world, the not-strictly-Jewish reality of the world, wanted to see Him]. In truth, I say to you, unless a grain of wheat fall to the ground and die, it remains just a grain of wheat; but if it dies, it produces much fruit [He had to die for the destiny of man, for the good of man]. Whoever loves his life loses it [he who is attached to himself loses himself] and whoever hates his life [whoever uses his life as a gift: hate is a Hebrew term that does not mean what it means for us] in this world will preserve it for eternal life. Whoever wants to serve me follows me, and where I am, there also will my servant be. And he will be honoured as the Father honours me. Now [in this moment] my soul is troubled [my soul, that of a

man, is troubled, is afraid: He knew they had to take Him].
Yet what should I say? … but if I came for this hour [if I
came in order to die! Now my soul is troubled, but what
should I say? But I came to die!]."

Note, then, the point: God was moved by our nothingness. Not only that. God was moved by our betrayal, by
our crude, forgetful, and treacherous poverty, by our pettiness. God was moved by our pettiness, which is even
more than being moved by our nothingness. "I have had
pity on your nothingness, I have had pity on your hatred
of me. I was moved because you hate me," like a father
and mother who cry with emotion because of their child's
hatred. They don't cry because they're struck, they cry
because they are moved, which means a cry that is totally
determined by the desire for the child's good, the child's
destiny: that the child may change, for his destiny, for the
child to be saved. It's compassion, pity, passion.

He had pity on me, the one who was so forgetful and
petty. If our life is normal, with what we've had, it is difficult to be able to find particular sins during the day, but *the*
sin is the pettiness of distraction and forgetfulness. The sin
is the pettiness of not translating what we do into something
new, not making it shine like the new dawn. Instead, we
leave it opaque, we leave it as it is, without striking anyone,
yet without giving it over to the splendour of Being.

He had pity on me and on my nothingness and He chose
me. He chose me because He had pity on me. He chose
me because He was moved by my pettiness!

What marks the devotion with which the Mystery – the
supreme Mystery and the Mystery of this man who is

Christ, God made man – what marks the Mystery's devotion to us, the devotion with which the Mystery creates the world and forgives man's pettiness, and forgives him while embracing him, embracing him who is petty, disgusting, is an emotion, it is like an emotion; it is being moved, it has being moved within it.

It is precisely this that exalts the maternity of God – as John Paul I says[19] – the maternal aspect of God, the feminine aspect of God (without overly stressing this, as they do nowadays, emptying it of serious content and turning it into nothing).

But remember that God's devotion to the world and to man is a theory that can be found in any pantheistic religion. In any pantheistic religion, God unites Himself to man and to the world to accomplish the order of the world, to accomplish the order of man, to accomplish the harmony of everything. It's a phrase that I heard the Buddhist monks use in Nagoya, Japan, when I went for a conference with them: "to accomplish the harmony of the world." When I went to this conference I described the concept of harmony – that exalted all the particulars, down to the hairs of the head (they exalt flowers, plants, but not the hairs of the head; but the hairs of the head are like flowers!) – which it has in common with Christianity, which Christianity understands and affirms. But in the last three minutes, I said that this harmony entered into the womb of a young woman and came out a man: a man. A man is the harmony of everything.

In all the other conceptions, this unity of God with the world and with man is stated in an arid and mechanical way. As with Dr Schweitzer: you must dedicate yourself, it is "your duty." This is like the champions of the Third World cause in the post-conciliar, post-World War II era: to go, to sacrifice yourself for humanity; it is your duty to go, it is not a case of being moved.

Being moved out of a judgment

We must pay attention to a particular point: this being moved and this emotion bear, bring with them, a judgment and a beat of the heart. It is a judgment, therefore a value, a rational value, let's say; not inasmuch as it can be boiled down and reduced to a level that only our reason is capable of, but rational in the sense that it gives a reason, it carries its reason within it. And it becomes a *beat of the heart* for this reason. If emotion or being moved doesn't carry this judgment and this beat of the heart within it, then it is not charity. What is the reason? "I have loved you with an eternal love, therefore I have made you part of me, having pity on your nothingness." The beat of the heart is pity on your nothingness – but the reason is that you might participate in being.

In talking about nothingness, as with an animal, you can use the term compassion. But when dealing with man – we'll conclude what I said before this way, by coming back to it – it can't be called anything but being moved, because man is called to happiness, man is great and is called to happiness; man is great like God and is called to God's happiness. The fact that he is crushed by pettiness, destroyed by distraction, emptied and turned into nothing again because of unlimited laziness, this generates compassion.

We have defined charity and we have described the two factors it is made of. It is a gift of self (devotion, a gift of self) until death. Christ's death reveals to us, unveils to us the totality of devotion with which the mystery of God dedicates Himself to our salvation. Being moved makes this self-giving of the Mystery, the gift of self that Christ accomplishes, unexpectedly human, unexpectedly and incomprehensibly human (even though it is incomprehensible it immediately feels human). Being moved at our life that is destined, as Thomas Mann says on the first page of *Joseph and His Brothers*: "This human life, by nature happy and against nature that is so unhappy." These aren't the exact words, but this is the concept.[20] Thomas Mann can write it with aesthetic emotion; God lived it to the point of death, because He was moved like a mother.

3 "PERFECT, LIKE YOUR HEAVENLY FATHER"

Now here is a third point, or, if you wish, a second part to our meditation.

We said that the word charity indicates the exact nature of God and therefore indicates the nature of all of the actions that God carries out and the relationships God establishes: a tender communication of self, giving being to everything, being moved.

Forty years ago when I was in Varigotti, a kitten fell from the second floor, flipped over a clothesline, and wound up crushed to a pulp on the ground; there, a few feet away, was the other kitten who was born with him. He remained there an instant staring at the other, then slowly walked away. This is the relationship between all men. It is only God who breaks through this estrangement and gives Himself to his creatures, bringing them out of nothing by His mercy, and continually re-fashioning them in an innocence full of the happiness of the dawn, because He is moved.

But now, first letter of John, chapter 4, verses 11–21: "Beloved, if God so loved us, we also must love one another. No one has ever seen God. Yet, if we love one another, God remains in us, and His love is brought to perfection in us. This is how we know that we remain in Him and He in us, that He has given us of His Spirit. And we have seen and testify that the Father sent His Son as saviour of the world. Whoever acknowledges that Jesus is the Son of God, God remains in him and he in God. We have come to know and to believe in the love God has for us. God is love, and whoever remains in love remains in God and God in him."

We must also love one another: morality is to imitate God in this; it is to follow Jesus or imitate the Father.

It's curious that in the gospel it says: "Be perfect, just as your heavenly Father is perfect."[21] Perfect like our Father: who is capable of that? This is a rash suggestion. As a suggestion it produces the opposite: fear. But a parallel passage in Saint Luke explains what it means: "Be merciful, just as your Father in the heavens is merciful."[22] Perfection is this being moved to action by man's need: his need for happiness, for being; for happiness, for destiny; for being, for destiny, for happiness.

It means being moved by the ultimate need of man: the "reason" that man is born. It would be wrong to bring children into the world if the destiny for happiness did not exist. I have said this since the first year I taught religion to freshmen in high school, and I challenged the students to tell me it wasn't true. Everyone was silent, everyone, even the most adversarial, even the active followers of Mondadori, even Angelo Rizzoli, even Del Pennino of the [Italian] Republican party, Strik Lievers, they were all the same age. And I said: "Do you have something to say?" and they were silent. It would be wrong to give birth if it were not for happiness, because giving birth would mean giving a child a possibility of atrocious suffering. The first among these sufferings is the absence of any meaning to his living, which he could escape only by being a fool. The ideal, therefore, for man to save himself, would be to be a fool.

We must follow Jesus and we must participate in the Father's mercy. When the Pope describes the mercy of God in his encyclical – which is this being moved by which God gives Himself to man, gives Himself to man to the point of dying for him – he says this mercy in history has a name: Jesus Christ.[23]

For this reason, after the first letter of John that I cited, you should read the first letter of Saint Paul to the Corinthians, the famous chapter thirteen: "If I speak the tongues of all men but do not have love [charity], I am a resounding gong or a clashing cymbal [I would not be a factor of universality, of ecumenism; even if I spoke the languages of all men and sustained everyone's ideas, I would not be ecumenical]. And if I have the gift of prophecy and comprehend all mysteries and all science [if I could explain everything], and if I possess the fullness of faith so as to move mountains [a strength of faith to move mountains] but do not have love [charity], I am nothing. If I give away everything I own, and if I hand my body over to be burned [Jan Palach anticipated[24]] but do not have love, I gain nothing."

Then what is it that you gain? What is this morality by which even giving your body over to be burned in flames for an ideal is useless, and being an Einstein serves no purpose, and being a Gandhi serves no purpose? What is this charity without which we are nothing? It is that the first object of man's charity is called Jesus Christ. Man's first object of love and of being moved is called "God made flesh for us," and because this Christ exists there is no longer any man who doesn't interest me. If only you could read certain notes of Mother Teresa and her sisters, especially one I often read a few years back that tells about how one of Mother Teresa's sisters found a man who was dying in a sewer in broad daylight. She took him, brought him home, washed him, got him in order, and that man said: "I lived like a wretch, now I'm dying like a king." But only a Christian can do this.

To love Christ and in Him, that is, according to His way, your brothers; devotion of self (gift of self) and being moved for others, for the other. So then, it is the I that affirms the you, it is the I that is fulfilled in affirming the you, it is the I that dies for the you. The drama is resolved.

Coki gave me this quote from Péguy, a quote that is moving to read: "As their freedom has been created in the image and likeness of my freedom, God says,/ As their freedom is the reflection of my freedom,/ So I love to find in them a certain gratuitousness. / A reflection of the gratuitousness of my Grace [grace is any movement with which God creates, because God's movement is creative]. As if created in the image and likeness of the gratuitousness of my Grace./ Thus I love in a certain way their praying not only freely but gratuitously./ I love their falling on their knees not only freely but gratuitously./ I love their giving of themselves and their heart and their picking up again and their bearing themselves and esteeming not only freely but gratuitously./ I love their loving after all, says God, not only freely but gratuitously./ Now for this, God says, I am well-served by my French./ They are a people who have come into the world with open hands and a liberal heart./ They give, they know how to give. By nature they are more easily gratuitous./ When they give, they don't see, they don't lend short-handedly and with high interest [they expect nothing in return, there is no recompense; moreover, if there is a recompense, they even give that away somewhere else, it makes them uncomfortable]/ They give for nothing. Otherwise is it giving?/ They love for nothing. Otherwise is it loving?"[25]

The truth of life is, therefore, affirming being. The object of every philosophy is also to affirm being, even when they negate it by a preconception that they introduce in principle. And this brings with it an affection, an attachment that can be hard as a rock. This affirmation of being, this affection for being can be hard as rock: "I have set my face like flint"[26] says God to the prophet Isaiah. It is hard as rock and cannot avoid being moved.

Another point, parenthetically: attachment to oneself does not exist if it is not based on being moved. Being moved unites while leaving one detached. To be truly moved, a person who is in love must be one metre, even two, away from the face of the beloved; and looking at that face, he is moved. Devotion to oneself doesn't exist if it isn't full of this movement, because in some way, one sees by moving out of oneself, abandoning oneself and moving oneself outwards to love. Otherwise you don't see love in the face of your beloved, not even in that face.

What is the wellspring, what is the source of this emotion and of this being moved, which we've discussed up until now and which we've insisted is necessary even for loving oneself, for affirming oneself? The source of this movement, in Christ, just as in myself, is the Spirit of Christ. The Spirit of Christ is the source of compassion and of being moved. That is why Christ calls Him the Consoler.

Your devotion and your being moved can be hard as rock; hard as rock, yet full of secret consolation. At this point, read the eighth chapter of the letter to the Romans; then read the passages in which Saint Paul describes his life in chapters four, five, six, and seven of the second letter to the Corinthians, and then tell me if there's a man who has greatness like Him, if a man like that can exist. He can exist! Because Mother Teresa is like that. He can exist! He can exist if he is fully moved for Christ and thus looks at man as Christ does: moved, thinking of his destiny and giving himself for his destiny, for man's destiny, for your destiny.

4 MORALITY IS TO IMITATE GOD IN CHARITY

Up until now, we've seen charity in its original value, which is identified with the blood of God, with the life of God. Charity is God.

We are born of God. First point: "The source of being is in You."

Try to imagine a baby who has just come to life in the womb of its mother, just conceived. To make an unimaginable paradox, if that small fetus knew that all that he is, everything, each tiny drop of blood, each cell from its newly begun structure, everything in him, comes from the body of his mother – and, in fact, that he is part of his mother's body as his mother's nose is part of his mother's body, as his mother's lung is part of his mother's body – if this small fetus could be aware, he would feel everything flowing from the organism of his mother: blood, nerves … Think of the kind of total dependence – total in the absolute sense of the term – his self-awareness must be, his consciousness of himself, this speck of reality, one cubic millimetre small: "The source of being is in you," he could say to his mother. "The source of being is in you."

Now, if charity is the dynamic law, the dynamism of that movement without end and without boundaries that is God (God is a movement of the gift of self, through His being moved, and He is determined by and lives this being moved), then everything that might be born from this sea of giving and being moved, the waters that flow from this infinite spring would have the same form, would have the same vibration, would have the same movement, would have the same dynamic, would have the same law. It would be charity.

Therefore, in his first letter, quoted last time, Saint John says: "If God so loved us, we must also love one another."[27] A relationship that is not of love does not exist, a true relationship does not exist if it is not one of love. That is what Jesus invites us to do in the gospel: "Be perfect as your Father is perfect." In the gospel we saw that "perfect" means merciful: you are gifts of yourselves also, fully moved, just as the immense flow of God's water is mercy, the immense flow of God's blood.[28]

How do you explain God's nature? How was it explained by Him, beyond all the images that human philosophies were able to build? As a source of being that gives itself totally. Thus the Son was generated, and in this relationship, a loving and moved energy just like theirs springs forth, which is the Holy Spirit. And, in fact, Saint John says *Deus caritas est*, God is love.[29]

What does it mean for us, we who are born of God – in which the source of our being is infinitely more than a mother for a baby in her womb – what does it mean that we must also love one another? If charity is described as a gift of self under the pressure of being moved, a gift of self charged with movement, it must be that way for us.

The law of the I – law is a description of the stable dynamism with which a reality strives towards its destiny, of the stable mechanism with which something in motion strives towards its goal – the dynamism proper to the I, which is therefore directly derived from the dynamism of God, is loving, that is, giving oneself to the other, being moved. There is no dynamism of the I without this.

Do you remember the sentence from Seneca: "If you want to live for yourself, you must live for another"? It means that if you want to live for yourself, if you want to fulfill your dynamism, you must live for another, you must give yourself to another, because you're moved, not because you're forced. It was the true intuition of a pagan.

This is the fundamental concept. Is it clear or not? Man comes from God – "the source of being is in You" – infinitely more than a baby is born from the viscera of his mother. While he is barely a speck in the viscera of his mother, his mother is everything, everything, in the literal sense of the word. If the baby were conscious of himself, he would say: "You are everything for me."

Therefore, since it comes from God, the I has love as its law. No other human law exists: you understand that the Gospel is divine because it's the only moral text … it is not only a text about morality, but it is the only text of morals in which morality is summed up in love. "Good teacher, what must I do?" the doctor of the law asks Him. And Jesus says: "How do you sum up the law?" "Love your neighbor as yourself."[30] The law of the I is one thing only: to love. And this is understandable because it is the law of the very source from which it is born: "The source of being is in You." God, who is the source of being, has only one dynamic, describable exclusively as gift of self, being moved.

In this way we are made part of and admitted to – slowly, slowly – the threshold of the great Mystery that makes all things, the Mystery of God the Father. God the Father loves by generating the Son, thus making the reality of the Spirit – which is identical to each of them – spring up in this relationship.

The law of the I is love, the law of the I is to give oneself.[31] When I was Prefect, and therefore sat at the desk in front of the high school class in the seminary, I was there to watch over the class. In it were two guys I cared for very much – two favourites – and I wrote entire notebooks on these things. To say that the law of the I is love means that the I doesn't exist, the I is not actualized, if not in love. And if it is not actualized in love, as love, the I is unsatisfied, angry with itself, hostile to others, incapable of taking in and assimilating the beauty of reality; it is bored, easily annoyed, etc. Go to the best dictionary and find synonyms for these words!

Gift of self to the end

Second thing: the measure of this law. Charity is the giving of self to the very depths. If there isn't the willingness to give oneself completely, the law is not applied.

For this reason love is true when it is eternal, when it is conceivable, accepted, desired as eternal: "No one loves as much as he who gives his life for his friends." Therefore, when one applies the law of love in the relationship with another in an authentic, true way, that is, open to going to the very depths, open to the endpoint, open to the ultimate, open to death and therefore to the eternal; when one gives himself to another in this way, he is everything for the other, everything. If the other knew how to reflect, looking at his friend with this loving openness towards him, he would tell him: "You are everything for me." It is exactly what Saint Paul said to Jesus: "It is no longer I who live, but it is You who live in me."[32]

Moving oneself for another

Third. But love for the other is not something generic, like a great, unexpected hot wind on certain spring days that makes us say: "Wow, summer is already here!" Devotion of oneself to another is not something generic, it's something very concrete. Why? Because the I is alive, not like a huge abstract cloud, but rather it lives as action; the I lives as action, it moves as action. My I wakes up, prays, eats, goes to work. A reality of nature that can say "I" is something that moves; if it moves, it goes from one position to another, it completes an act, it determines its own evolution.

Therefore, if the law of the I is giving oneself, love as giving oneself to another, giving oneself to another means moving oneself for another.

You can be there, enchanted, looking at a beautiful painting of Saint Dominic by Fra Angelico on the wall there in the back. But if that friar were seated here in front and Luca, playing ball here, were to jump back and come close to knocking thoughtful Saint Dominic over ... if I love this poor man, I run ahead to stop Luca. Do you get what I mean? To love someone means to move. Imagine a mother who "loves" her child; but if the child gets sick, she doesn't move even one inch because she "is a little lazy." The baby can die ... with a mother who "loves him very much"! To give oneself to others means to move oneself for others.

To bring into being, to save

At this point it is easier to understand the fundamental question: to move for what? In the preceding case, it was at least to save Saint Dominic's hide from Luca's fury. Move for what? Why does one give oneself to another? What did Seneca say? "It is necessary to live for another in order to live for oneself." To live for another, what does that mean? Why do we live for another? And for ourselves, too, what does it mean? I understand if one were to say: to live for another so that I put a million and a half a month in my pocket ... aside from the fact that, after ten months, I don't know what to do with it, except stay there every night counting it!

For what reason does a mother give herself to her son? "Eat more, eat more fruit ...": to make her devotion to her son more substantial, but what for? To make him grow, right? But grow, for what? To make him become himself, to make him become a man! And then? In religious language, one would say "to redeem him." What does it mean to say that a mother redeems her child? To redeem means to bring into being, that is, to save. In Latin, "save" means to preserve. Preserve him for what? So that he is fulfilled, so that he be completely himself and therefore so that he be eternal. Without the word "eternal" an I no longer becomes itself and even less does it become fulfilled.

Let's sum up all we've said on all these points, each of which invites us to complete a specific step. Man exists to affirm Another, Another who is called God. This is the truth that moves the heart, moves it and makes it act. True love, that is, the true fulfillment of the law of man, which is the aim of living, is to affirm Being, is to affirm the Other, is "to affirm You, God." Analogously, to dedicate oneself to one's brother, to another person, to act for another, to be moved for another, is true love inasmuch as it desires that the other know the truth and live the truth of his being in a complete way. In other words, true love is looking at another and treating another with the desire that he become true, that he fulfill his destiny. Without love for destiny there is no love, without love for the destiny of another there is no love for another.

There is something truly moving that we have often said: a mother who has never looked at her child from one, two, or three metres away, and, as she sees him play or sees him write at the desk where he does his homework, has never thought, "What is awaiting this child? Why have

I had this child? Why does this child study? Why does this child play? Why does this child eat? Why does this child get big?" and has never, with a start, perceived that she does all this for her child's happiness, that is, for that child's eternal destiny, that mother has never loved her child in the true womanly way, in the true human way.

To desire your destiny. You can have so many degrees of emotion when you say this, yet they all have a common denominator: the desire for the destiny of the other. So much so that He who loved men most died on the cross for their destiny.

In the notes on this lesson from last year there is a sentence that needs to be changed. The sentence reads: "A person truly loves another when he detaches himself from that person and sees in that other the possession of Another, that is, of God." He doesn't "detach himself from that person," but "goes to the depths of that person," because love, to the degree that it ends in eternity, loses nothing, not even a hair from the head, as Jesus said, not even a small breeze that is barely heard.

One loves when, in some way, one desires destiny. When you give five dollars to the African who is standing on the curb, you give it to him for his destiny, thinking of his destiny. If you buy the rose they bring you in the square some evening, it isn't for what the person who sells it to you slyly thinks – to simply give it to the driver who drives your car – but it's to give the seller money. Anyway, putting a rose with thorns into the hand of the driver of your car … !

A different kind of life

The application of the law of love, this supreme imitation of God, sooner or later determines a different kind of life.

This different kind of life doesn't mean faultlessness: one can make a thousand mistakes, but his life is different. Above all, a person bears the sorrow for his mistakes, for what he forgets. In everything he does, he brings the sign of a change, of which sorrow for a love not well-realized is the sharpest example; no one in the world has this kind of sorrow. Aside from one who is aware of these things that Jesus brought and that the apostles brought to the world, the others don't know this sorrow at all.

Let's make a list of the aspects of this new form of relationship among people, the aspects of this change that can take place, the aspects of this difference that occurs in life.

First. The affirmation of another because he is and for how he is: not for our own profit, for our own calculation, nor for the way we would like him to be. Affirmation of another as he is, because he is: this is the true esteem that belongs to man.

Second. Sharing needs. Through need man is pushed toward his destiny; through need he learns he lacks something. To share needs means to catch yourself realizing that you are a loving presence whose interest is the destiny of the other just as much as your own destiny.

Third. Forgiveness, capacity for forgiveness, which means to give back space and freedom within yourself to the other.

Someone offended you: he is excluded from connection to you. Forgiveness is to let him enter in again: you give him back space and freedom.

Fourth. Attachment to the other, affection for man; both as devotion (respect), and as faithfulness (continuity of respect).

To the degree to which these new attitudes are at work in man, two other things occur, which concisely express the possible change in man.

First, a change of mentality comes about. One who applies these things on a streetcar, behind the bureaucrat's desk, in the professor's chair, or as father or mother, demonstrates a mentality that is different from that of others. He who works this way brings about a change of mentality whose most beautiful description is in the Letter to the Romans, twelfth chapter, verses 1 and 2, which we old folks remember fondly because the comment on these two verses of Saint Paul was the object of an "Open Letter to the Christians of the West" by a great Czechoslovak theologian, persecuted by the regime and jailed for twelve years, whose name was Zverina.[33] In this passage, he even analyses the weight of the words in Greek: change – he says – change your mind, change your mentality, your way of reasoning, the categories of reasoning; do this to change your hearts: it will bring about a metamorphosis of your hearts.

What is the principal fruit of this change of mentality, the normal mentality, occurring in a thousand out of a thousand men? What is it like? To earn, to save, to enjoy, to like, to succeed? The apex of this change of mentality is the offering of one's own life: if love is the law of life, the apex is to offer it.

CHARITY: ASSEMBLY

This is the way you should be working on our lessons: grasp the meaning of the lesson in its entirety, not in an analytical sense, but as a complete world; understand the reasoning behind the individual passages; understand it sentence by sentence; then look back and say, "Wonderful! Nobody says these things like this."

Instead, if you sit there, alone or in a group, reading the text line by line until you come across something objectionable and you raise your hand, you run the risk of splitting the lesson up rather than unifying it. Instead of envisioning a world, of being awestruck by a new world, you create many fragments that are difficult to piece together, like a puzzle. Whereas the world embraces many things and is one voice.

You spoke of how God is moved for man and of the judgment that this being moved bears. Can you explain this judgment better?
Here's the first part of the answer: God knows that we are made for happiness, that man is made for happiness. It's like going into a hospital ward and seeing a child whose leg has been badly mangled by a car. That child was made to have two limbs and run around. So when someone passes by that small bed, they are moved. This is the real reason, although it may never be verbalized: this poor child had two legs to

run and play with, and now they will have to amputate. The reason for God's *compassion* toward man is this: man is made for happiness and his miserable state of sin or weariness or ignorance impedes him; it tends to impede his happiness. Therefore, God's pity is full of reason. "God has pity on man," God's love for man is fully moved, and this being moved has a reason: God sees that man is made for happiness and that he is prey to temptation, weakness, and confusion that impede his happiness, that slow him down, that make it more difficult. God's compassion towards man, then, becomes God's being moved; he comes close to man and says, "Take heart, I will go with you."

Isn't this also because being moved is the most original position and therefore the most reasonable position with respect to reality?
For a position to be reasonable, there must be a reason for it. What is the reason? You are using an expression that, while not contradictory, is different from the one we used. You say that being moved is the first sentiment that one has of reality. I say that the first sentiment one has towards reality is curiosity, not compassion. Perhaps is it even wonder towards something greater; but not compassion, which is a sentiment one has towards something smaller than oneself.

What has to happen for wonder to become being moved?
Wonder – it is something wonderful that man is made for complete happiness – becomes being moved when something exists that might impede this happiness, that is an enemy to happiness (then being moved helps man overcome this obstacle.)

Wonder becomes being moved when the heart of God or of the person judging becomes one with the heart of man and experiences all his desire. It's not just wonder, but the emotion of participating in a desire for which man justly struggles, which man knows how to await with patience.

You see a beggar standing at the curbside, on the corner, always in the same spot, leaning against the wall, with one leg bent underneath and his hand out. You go by in the morning and you see him there, you pass by in the evening and you see him there. In the morning you say, "Poor fellow, he has the right to some money, too." When you pass him in the evening you get a lump in your throat because you are moved at the thought that he stood there all day. You see?

Man begins his journey and this journey evokes wonder because at the end lies happiness, destiny; days, months, and years pass and he has to overcome many difficulties, lies, confusion, errors – he has to continually overcome himself. So you wonder not only at the fact that he is made for an eternal destiny, but you are moved because he has to overcome many trials to reach his destiny.

When as a child I started to draw and I was not very good (not like those geniuses who get it right away), my father used to come home from work and stand behind me and watch me. The first feeling that he had was undoubtedly, "He has do it, if they gave him this task to do, he has to do it." I would draw, then erase, then draw, then erase. If my father loves me, he thinks, "Poor kid." So he intervenes and says, "Make this line this way, not that way."

You see? He intervenes because he has compassion, though the initial attitude was a judgment: "He must do it."

You said that in charity one acts out of pure love for another and out of love for his destiny. I would like to propose this very simple, mundane example. At my job, I work with people who are older than me, and they sometimes take advantage of me by saying, "Do this," just because they don't want to do it. In that moment, I wonder what charity means with respect to a person like that at work.

Not just in that moment, always!

My first reaction is to say, "Absolutely not."

And this would be human justice.

On the other hand, I wonder what does pure love for another, love for his destiny, mean for me. I realize that it's not easy to fully understand the reasons for these things …

There are no reasons, there is no reason why someone who has a job to do should tell another, "Do it." "Why? What do you take me for?" It's precisely because there is no reason that if you do it, it becomes charity. It can become stupidity or it can become charity.

Charity poses itself in the relationship with another when there is no reason, no return, no calculation − as normally happens in every initiative man takes with regard to someone else. The only reason is because that man is loved by God, although he is a man, and so he is prey to laziness.

O.K. you help him up to a certain point. If he asks me a second or third time, I say yes. After the third time, it would take Father Kolbe – you would need a halo! Can someone go on forever like this? Yes, if he knows how to walk the road Jesus walked.

Charity is a service given without calculating, without return, to make the path easier for another. If, instead, he asks you to do his job because he wants to go watch a movie, you tell him, "Look, do it yourself" (otherwise you're not making his path any easier for him).

To make another's path easier means to help him feel his destiny more, help him not to feel alone in his difficulty. For example, a woman died last night, a woman whom many of you here know (she was one of the first in the group Gioventù Studentesca). She was always surrounded by friends. What did these friends gain from her? Nothing; it was gratuitous, you see. This is charity. If her husband the lawyer had given each person who came for an hour twenty-five dollars, the connotations of the value of the visit would have changed.

You said that the primary object of man's charity, love, his being moved is "God became man for him," and that because Christ exists, I am interested in every man. I would like to understand better what it means to say that Christ is the primary object of love.

What partner, what encounter can be reason enough for the total gift of self? If someone says, "If I were to meet a beautiful girl, so beautiful that there is no one more beautiful than she is, I would say to her, 'My Lady, I dedicate my life to you,'" he is like a dog on a leash. We are talking about a young girl who four years from now withers and we must say of her, "Read between the wrinkles," as the humorist Clericetti says in one of his saddest expressions.[34]

The conversion of Saint Francis Borgia came about like this: Queen Isabelle, the wife of Charles V, one of the most intelligent and powerful women in Spain at the time, had died. Francis Borgia assisted in transporting her exhumed body to the cathedral. He was converted upon seeing that cadaver filled with worms.

If, instead, of Isabelle of Portugal, we speak of God made man − Beauty with a capital B, the font of Beauty, as Leopardi would say − then who is worthy of the attention that would actively spark our wonder, to the point that we want to consecrate our lives to him, our whole life for him? Who is more worthy than this man? This is what some people felt as they looked at Christ; this is what came to mind looking at Him! The primary object of charity as the gift of self, as being moved … just as it is moving to realize that the most beautiful person in the world exists among us (read the beginning of Psalm 44). Not only is He beauty made man, someone that you can encounter on the street, who keeps company with us every day, He is also so good that He gives His life for us, He gives His life for me. And just as He gives it for me, He gives it for you, and He gives His life for the train conductor that I don't even know, and for the German SS officer who killed the partisans at Fosse Ardeatine − He gives his life for all.

On the one hand, the first charity is towards Him; on the other hand, this charity tends to touch every man, any man more easily evokes our compassion.

Nowadays, while I am working, I strive to think about what
has been said here and this has resulted in two things: first, an
exasperated energy inside me; and second, I realized that there
was a single criterion at the base of my life: I could see myself
with my needs in the balance at that moment, in that place.
This really impressed me.

Our friend has given us a beautiful witness, because
nurturing this thought, or better yet, living this memory
of Christ, first makes the will to live grow – he used the
word "exasperated," "exasperated energy" – an intense will
to live. Second, it generates a unity in life. Life has unity
when it has a goal. A path is made up of millions of steps,
but it is "a" path if it has "a" goal. Therefore, this witness
that a certain thought, as we have expressed it, about what
Christ is for man and about the virtue that is the greatest
for man – charity – first makes life richer in "affectus,"
affection. Here, "exasperated" means "loaded with affection." Second, it makes life more reasonable because it is
unified. This is precisely where our whole discourse leads,
what we say with the School of Community, everything
we have been saying in the Movement for forty years. He
who follows Christ has eternal life and one-hundred-fold
here below, one-hundred-fold in affection and reason,
unity in reason.

My question is on the Epistle to the Corinthians. I want to
better understand the part when Christ says, "Without charity
I am nothing, without charity nothing is useful." Oh no, it was
Saint Paul who said it.

It makes no difference. If I don't have this kind of openness, which is full of wonder and therefore full of the urge to give, of offering, of being moved at Being made man – at the Mystery of Being that makes the stars, the sea, everything, which has become man – if I am not profoundly moved, nothing has meaning, nothing is of any use to me. I can be moved in one moment, but a moment later … as the poet whom I always quote says, "What you seek most to grasp and hold tight in your hand comes undone like the rose under the gaze of eternity."[35] Like the rose under the gaze of eternity that withers day after day and in the evening is no longer as it was in the morning, what you seek most to grasp and hold tight in your hand has come undone, you haven't possessed it, you have destroyed it. In order not to destroy it, you need a rose you can hold by its stem, that you can look upon with admiration, bathed in the morning dew and fed by the mysterious winds of the Mystery of Being. Then the rose will last for eternity. Ideally it will last for eternity, it won't wither. So, faced with all of the difficulties in life – and every day is full of difficulty – as we look at others, we understand all of the suffering they must endure. You understand their suffering, even though they do not realize it themselves! When you are on the train and you look around at the people with all the burdens they bear, you see their burdens and they do not even realize it, they don't even think about it, because if they did they would begin to curse.

While you were explaining charity and gratuitousness, I was thinking that, of all the things I heard this year, this is what

*most deeply moved me; that is, this is what I really want from
my day: a gratuitous way of being with people and things.*

*At the same time, however, this week I saw how this is the thing
that I am least capable of. In the end, it's as if my gratuitousness
became a non-loving, that is, a non-affection; as if in order to be
gratuitous, I became almost cold. Instead, what you were saying
was the ability to love the person in front of you more strongly,
and I am not able to do this.*

None of us is able to be himself, that is, to be true, without
holding his hand out and begging God to bring to comple-
tion what he has begun: "God, you began this good work
that bears my first and last name, bring me to comple-
tion."[36] Being capable of charity means to be able to look
at people, treat people, to look at and treat things as God
looks at them and treats them. But it's difficult. You said
two very correct and beautiful things. First, charity is the
most beautiful theme of the entire year (the most impressive theme is faith, and underneath it all, emerging from
the darkness, you understand that there is a Presence in the
darkness. If you accept this Presence in the darkness, the
idea of charity is also awakened.) We are not capable of
charity without the help of God; therefore, the greatest
action a man can take is to beg, like that fellow on the street
corner, resting on one leg up against the wall, holding his
hand out from morning to night and until the morning
comes again (something like what Pascoli's blind man intu-
its as the answer, although in a negative sense. Do you
remember Pascoli's blind man?[37]).

There's something I need to understand.

Well, asking in order to understand is a sign of intelligence; after all, a goose doesn't ask in order to understand.

When you spoke about giving without expecting something in return, it made me think about what was said during the lesson on obedience. We were told that obedience would lead to something more in life and then we were told to read that piece of the Gospel where Christ prayed for His glory. So I would like to understand what this has to do with getting nothing in return.

Whatever you do out of charity, you do without expecting a return – don't even think about what you get in return – you do it to give of yourself, out of being moved and out of wonder. A return is something that comes at the end and reveals the reasonableness and the justice of charity; because of your charity you will receive a hundredfold, but that's not why you act. If you count on having the hundredfold, you will lose what little you have. Anyway, what moved Christ to ask was his love for the truth as established by the Father, not his vainglory.

What is the difference between compassion and being profoundly moved?

I made an analogy. When I was sick – just after becoming a priest I was sick for three years – I lived in this hospice run by the nuns together with a rather cunning friend of mine who later became a priest himself. We used to chase after the cats. Once there were two newborn cats. One was down in the garden and the other was playing somewhere above when he fell and splattered on the ground, though not on account of us. The other cat, his companion, stood still, looking at him for, I don't know, some seven or eight seconds. Then he slowly went away, nonchalantly. This is compassion: a reaction proportionate to the awful occurrence. You are passing by on the highway at 170 kilometres per hour and you see on the side of the road – there are many people on the side of the road – a woman lying on the ground – pale, dead. You have compassion, a reaction of equal proportion to this horrible accident.

Being profoundly moved is something that touches you, moves you and, where possible, makes you do something. If you had stopped your car and run over there saying, "Do you need help? I am a doctor, do you need something? Have you called the police?" "No." "Does anyone have a cellular phone?" "I have one." So you grab the phone and wait there; you spend an hour, maybe even two or three – then this is real, this is being moved. So I said – just to make it short – you have compassion toward animals and are moved by people. Can you talk about being moved when a dog gets run over by a car? No, but compassion, yes.

You told us that a heartbeat is not charity if it has no reason and the reason is my participation in being. What does participation in being mean?
Participating in being? Participation in being is the object of your consciousness, of your awareness, because you are, you exist. Existing means participating in being. You did not give yourself existence, it was given to you, you were given the gift of existence. When your mother was expecting you, quite probably – and I say probably because everything is possible in this dog-eat-dog world, this cynical

world, cynical meaning "canine" – your mother said, "He is a gift from God." If she didn't say this, it's because – excuse this hypothesis – she didn't believe in God. Anyway, there was recognition of something, of the universe, of the mystery of things. You participate in being, you exist because you were made to participate in something else that already exists. What exactly was your question?

I really wanted to understand what it means to say that a heartbeat isn't charity if there is no reason and the reason is so that I may participate in being.

Once I am aware that you participate in being, I am ready to feel emotion or I am moved when I meet you or when something happens to you. Emotion or being moved is directed towards something that exists, and it exists because an Other exists. You were not made by yourself. This is the reason for living: the reason for living is what we are made for, what you are made of, the reason for living is an Other. If you were to use everyday language, you would say that you are on a first name basis with this Other: the familiarity of the word "you" expresses in a supreme way, a synthetic and supreme way, the awareness of a Presence that made you, because before you did not exist and you don't make yourself be. "I am You-who-make-me," says chapter ten of *The Religious Sense*, which is the greatest, most calming, most moving, most awe-inspiring and beautiful discovery one can make.[38]

You said that ...

This "you" that you use in a formal way is really a familiar "you." If the formal use of the pronoun "you" is not used as substitution for a familiar "you," it separates us, it doesn't let you reach the other person, therefore you really don't understand whom you are talking to.

You said that charity is the most profound and mysterious part of that Presence that we know by faith, and this cannot be understood, it can only be followed. And then right afterwards you said that charity produces an effect and changes things through experience; moreover, that charity speaks to the heart with authority and responds to the needs that constitute the heart. I would like to understand the nature of this supreme experience that allows us to understand charity and what you mean when you say that reason must follow what this experience brings?
What allows us to understand charity in a supreme way is probing the mystery, which can be measured by the wavelength known as eternity. In eternity, paradise won't be a sort of deathly boredom where the same things repeat themselves over and over again. It will be a long road where every moment is different, new, an event – as the journalist who wrote about Péguy said.[39] An event is something new, an event is fundamental for knowing; you gain knowledge when you learn something new.

So, in a supreme way, charity is an experience of the infinite, the eternal. You begin when you are a baby and you never stop. Charity is the measure of your destiny, what you were made for.

What was your second question?

What do you mean, in this case, that reason must follow?
What is reason? Man's capacity to become aware of reality.
Does that mean that reality comes from man or that he is
able to create reality? No, it means that he becomes aware
of something that he does not make. It's the same here. In
obedience, you become aware of a Presence so mysterious
that to know it you must follow him who knows already,
step by step, forever. Therefore, obedience understood as
following him who already knows is intelligence – climb-
ing a mountain while following someone who knows
nothing is stupid.

But who already knows that infinite horizon to which
you can truly apply the word love (pure love, not calculating, without return, without measure)? God made man,
Christ, and those who Christ has put next to you so that
you might follow Him, enlightening them so that they
help you to follow Him.[40]

*You said that the truth of life is to affirm being and that this
bears an affection, an attachment that, although it may be hard
as stone, cannot avoid being moved.*
How beautiful! Why are you laughing? Because I said it?
Why no, I didn't say it. It was also told to me. As you grow
older, you understand that everything true that exists is a
gift. The great task remains: your freedom must accept it;
you must accept it with all its consequences as they are
slowly revealed. You can love a person, even with enthu-
siasm, purely, justly – yet as you progress, the implication
of sacrifice emerges, ever imposing itself until, when God
wishes, it covers everything. This is the moment when the

resurrection is near, that is, when the stability of truth made certain, which is totally useful, totally yours, draws near.

I would like to understand what is meant by an attachment that can be as hard as stone that cannot avoid being moved.
The truth of life lies in affirming being; affirming the existence of a beautiful chrysanthemum; that beautiful chrysanthemum is bigger than your hand, and its stem struggles to support it because it's so big, so true, so beautiful. You behold it and you are moved. If you were to look at that chrysanthemum and say, "Well, maybe it doesn't exist, maybe it's just an impression. Maybe it's my mother, maybe it's my son," you no longer love anything – only a "doctrine" can constantly use the word "maybe."

Is that what you were saying about modern philosophy, which denies the concreteness of being, the concreteness of reality, relegating it to fantasy because reality appears to be an enemy?
Certainly. If reality is different from what evidence presents, it's a lie, an enemy. Think of 1912 in Libya when the Arabs, who didn't have cannons as we Italians did, made enormous ditches and covered them with leaves. Our soldiers came along with their artillery and fell right in. What appears as evident, but is not true, is deception, and deception is the product of an enemy.

At first, one's affection can be arid and therefore as hard a stone, one's attachment can be hard, but with time, it is moved.
So you shouldn't be worried about it, if at first you are not moved.

The first thing to worry about is whether something is to be loved or not. If it is a lie, I cannot love it. There's nothing hard or soft about it, or rather, when faced with a lie, one tends to be soft because the characteristics with which a lie presents itself are easier to swallow. On the other hand, if your mother loves you and she tells you to do something right, and you don't want to do it, you stand in front of her with your stone face. If you do what she asks you will, in time, learn, and say to her, "Mother, you were so right." (Now that she is dead).

I would like to start from a small incident that occurred to me. The other day, I was a little late getting to work and a colleague of mine left this note on my desk, "A good day for me starts with the fact that we meet each other, that we see each other. Since I cannot see you, I will write you." Since our discussions are usually a bit empty, I was really happy that she might have intuited the possibility of a more profound correspondence in a relationship. In defining charity, you said that you act out of pure love, as if one didn't have to expect this correspondence in a relationship. Instead, for me, it's important that the other person recognize it.
You were late for work and she didn't see you …

No, she left me a message saying, "A good day for me starts with the fact that we meet each other, that we see each other …"
Because you were late, she didn't see you!

Yes, but …
But this has more to do with the question than it seems to you. In fact, she goes on to say … ?

So she left me this note saying, "I just wanted to tell you,"
and I was moved because I understood there could be a deeper
correspondence in our relationship. I know, even though she may
not recognize it or understand it very well, that this is the
beginning of the possibility of a truer relationship,
of correspondence.

You discovered the possibility of a correspondence between you and your co-worker that you weren't expecting. When she had the chance to tell you this because you were late and this is an extremely important sign. It's as if your friend told you, "You may have many different reasons for being late, but if you are late, you impede me from starting my day well." The way to better conform to the correspondence she showed you was to show that you, too, were anxious to see her, that is, anxious to get there on time. Your happiness is only half true; it's missing that sacrifice of self in order to complete it, to make it useful, for happiness to coincide with *pure love.*

You said, "If you belong to an Other, life is dramatic." I want to know what dramatic means.

Besides the fact that we are talking about a word, a word like "seat" for example. ("I want to know what a seat is." "A seat is that thing you sit on and lean back against.")

Dramatic points to a precise phenomenon, the phenomenon whereby an "I" addresses "another" as "you." An I that says "you" to another must overcome all of the differences before crossing the threshold of the initial beatitude; the joy of being in a relationship must first purify the relationship of what doesn't correspond.

Since the lack of correspondence is normal – it's normal that between one person and another there is no correspondence – such correspondence must be desired in order to enter into a friendship and into the peace of a relationship with another person. Wanting this correspondence is a struggle, a difficulty. In this sense, every relationship between two people is dramatic and the most difficult element of this drama lies in the difference (between you) that must be honestly recognized but accepted and burnt away by the will to love. There are many phenomena: recognizing, accepting, burning – there is even a fire!)

Between God the Father, the Word, and the Holy Spirit there is no drama, except with respect to the outcome of creation, to their relationship with creation. There is no drama between them because the unity of love is so total that it doesn't allow for any difference – like father, like son. The drama begins with the energy expressed in creation; the drama doesn't begin among them, it begins at our level. Everyone was following the Son with their mouths agape, hoping to partake in some little miracle. Whether a miracle occurred or did not occur, however, was a result of the Father's will. To our eyes and in our experience, the relationship between the Father and Son seems dramatic because it is a relationship that provokes and generates contrast, not correspondence.

One must strive towards correspondence, like that between the Father and Son. What is dramatic is man's existence at his origin – in his originality – dramatic, too, is his solemn march toward his destiny. Only at his destiny will this drama be assuaged.

How is charity toward oneself possible? If I realize that Christ loved me so much that he died for me, this step should be more immediate, yet I have trouble being charitable toward myself.

Do you remember the line from Dante, "This precious jewel, upon the which is every virtue founded, Whence hadst thou it?"[41] To be virtuous, to fight within the drama of a relationship, you must have the result of joy within you. Without having experienced joy, you can't do it very well. "This dear joy upon which all virtue is founded, from whence does it come to you?" You have joy in you that comes from something that makes your virtue, your desire for good, begin to stir. What is this joy and from where do you get it? This joy is your desire for happiness. Where does it come from? It comes from your origin, from Him who made you. Therefore, the desire for happiness in you is based on the fact that you were made for happiness; He who created you made you for happiness, and so you cannot help desiring your happiness.

I want to better understand what is the meaning of "The principal fruit of a change in mentality is the offering of your very life," because during the day I either follow my illusions or I recognize that I am in front of Christ.

She sees that in every moment of her life she either follows her illusions – meaning, what she does and thinks is wrong, vain, empty – or it's for Jesus. In other words, what she does is either useless or worthwhile. If it's worthwhile, if it has substance, if it's important in the year 1220 or in 1994, it's because it belongs to Christ. Either it's useless, and so what was worthwhile in December 1111 is no longer worth anything in February 1112, or it's for Jesus. When something is done for Jesus, it lasts, it's useful for man, it lights his way and gives him a foretaste of everlasting joy and gladness.

So, what was your question?

Can you explain this part of the lesson better?
Not as I did the last time!

No, I certainly didn't mean it like that.
Don't correct yourself because you're right. Otherwise of what use is the time that passes and our repeating things? No use. If it's for Jesus, the passing of time and repetition are creative.

The principal fruit of this change of mentality is the offering of your very life.
The change in mentality is the most impressive and meaningful factor of life perceived as a passage, life that passes. When my father dragged me around the various churches in Lombardy to hear the polyphonic music they would play on Sundays (Palestrina and others), I didn't go along very willingly. Polyphonic music – I hope you know what it is: music where everything is confused! – seemed like a jumble of words and notes. When I was in my third year of high school, in the seminary, that Good Friday when I heard the beginning of De Victoria's *Caligaverunt* – the same one we sing today – as soon as the second voice joined in, I no longer perceived this confusion.[42] I understood what polyphonic music was. And the more the other

parts joined in, the third and fourth voices, the more beautiful it became. It was no longer a mess. This represents a change in mentality.

If you listen to music in an immature fashion, you won't understand a thing; if you listen to it in a more mature way, you will begin to understand. The more you listen, the more you will understand. It's a rather prodigious thing: the more complicated the piece is and the more you struggle with it, the more it reveals itself to you, it unfolds before you. If it is composed of six vocal parts, the more you listen to it and think about it, the more these six voices begin to unravel — you hear the first part, the second, third, fourth, the fourth repeats itself, the fifth — this is maturity. A musician understands it in this way, forget about the musician! The adult person for whom music was made (music was made for man, not for the musician) understands!

The change in mentality means better understanding the nature of a phenomenon — the factors that constitute it — and perceiving more clearly the function that all these factors have in achieving an ultimate goal. The meaning of the goal is the height of the human spirit; everything is destined for this goal. As in Mont Blanc where that enormous heap of stuff ends in a peak, everything is in service of the peak. This is the first thing I want to point out: a change in mentality signifies a deeper and more detailed understanding of the factors that make up something as a function of its unique and ultimate meaning. Think about the map of the world that Ptolemy drew, as opposed to the expert maps drawn today. They are two very different things. Today's map reveals a development of mentality.

A change in mentality means penetrating the heart of the factors that make up a phenomenon in a more detailed way; it's a more acute perception of the one goal towards which everything flows, for which all these factors were made. (Whatever doesn't flow towards the one goal is like veinstone, waste, that must be thrown away.)

What does offering your day to God mean? Man, meaning nature's highest expression – nature's height of expression including the heavens and the stars, white or withered rose gardens, heaven and earth – man is the height of heaven and earth. When we sing in the preface of the liturgy, "All the earth shouts your praise," where does the earth shout? It is man who shouts, who gives voice to, who is the awareness of all the earth. In offering his day, man reveals having reached a deeper awareness of the factors that make up reality and of the one destiny these factors were made for. The one destiny they were made for is the glory of Christ. "Father, my hour has come" – another of the most beautiful pieces in the Gospel; just think about this. He said it an hour before being arrested – "Father, my hour has come, glorify your Son."[43] The greatness of all reality, just like the top of Mont Blanc, is the glory of Christ. All the factors in reality that you become aware of ... the more you mature the more you understand that the sole purpose for the existence of all these factors is to affirm Christ.

Why is the affirmation of Christ the sole purpose for the existence of the factors that make up reality, why is it the reason that even a single hair on you head is important, as the Song of Songs would put it, "You struck me with a single strand of your hair"?[44] Why is the glory of Christ the goal of all these things? When I was a child, I was very much impressed by this thought that came to me in the pine forest, "How many pine needles there are in these trees!" I would start to count them: ten, twenty, forty, one hundred – I'd get bored by the time I reached a hundred – and a hundred was nothing. On just one tree there must have been thousands, and with all the pine trees in the world? Millions and millions of needles. And this is just one factor, just one; what about the grains of sand on the beach? The pinnacle of the sum of all things that make up reality – the pinnacle, the final destination, the ultimate goal – is the glory of Christ. Because all things are made of Christ. Your hair didn't exist, not even that one strand that struck your heart. Your hair didn't exist, nor did your eyes – and if you had no eyes … ! But most of all your heart didn't exist, meaning there was nothing. Everything that you are made of, everything, everything consists in Him; it is made of something that doesn't come out of nowhere. "Out of nowhere" there is Being and there is only one Being: the Mystery of God who was made man. So everything is the glory of Christ, because everything is made of Christ. We have always said that to offer something to God means "God I offer this hour of study to you" (like our friend Anna who is forced to study on the train, in churches, and in train station cafes because she is studying medicine and has to study twenty-four hours a day to pass one exam at a time, even Physiology). Anyway, what does "I offer you this hour of studying on the train" mean? (Always the same thing, what a pain!) That what I do consists of You, is made of You, is made of Something Else, everything is made of Something Else, everything is made of You, and the purpose of everything is the glory of this You. This You reveals itself in the very form of my action. "Glory" means the reverberation of the countenance of this You. The stars exist to reveal the face of Christ, and thank God, there are things in existence other than withered or white roses to reveal the face of Christ.

A change in mentality is that event of maturity whereby, with the passing of time, one's awareness of what all things are made of (and the more beautiful they are, the more they are made of that substance) and of the purpose for which they were made (which is that the face of Christ be revealed in them) becomes habitual. Understanding music is not habitual for a child; what moves the father says nothing to the child, but when the child grows up, he will also be moved. Therefore, the supreme value of the change in mentality lies in offering everything to Christ. That means recognizing that everything is made of You and that everything is made to reveal You. In fact, this is the only thing that can fill the heart and soul with gladness, even in the face of suffering, even in the face of death. Like my friend Vannini's father who, on his deathbed with all his loved ones gathered around, raised his hand with great difficulty and said, "Until we meet again." How many stories like this can we tell?

A change in mentality means to go from being a child to being an adult; to understand the world, to make full use of the world or to enjoy the world, to enjoy being. There is nothing than makes you understand the truth of the world and enjoy it fully like offering. The height of maturity is making an offering to God. Offering something to God means recognizing that what we are handling is made of Him, that our action is accomplished by Another, is made of Another. It is not accomplished by me, who am nothing; everything is given to me and is done by me "for," so that the different voices of the polyphonic piece are revealed, so that, one by one, the features of the face of Christ are revealed.

When we are young, we don't understand anything and everything seems abstract. It is the same for the child: apart from his food and the person feeding him, everything else is abstract. But when he grows to be six, ten, fourteen, twenty, forty years old, until that time he may still be somewhat of a child – this I have recognized in our own people, they are children until they are forty years old – after that they bottom out; either they bottom out, which means they sleep (all the time!), things weigh them down, time weighs them down, events weigh them down, or they begin to understand.

You said that the law of the "I" is love. The "I" is not something abstract but moves in action, so to give yourself to another means to move for another. I am tempted to ask: when is this lived in a moralistic way, something I measure, a force of will? When your reason for action is not the love for another but a law that you were taught, a law that you learned, a formula you learned. My late mother used to come and tuck me in every night, every single night until I was ten years old and I went into the seminary – then I no longer had my mother to watch over me; priests are not mothers. While she was tucking in the bed sheets, every night she would say something different: if it were raining, "Remember those children who don't have a roof over their heads, or a warm room to sleep in as we do" or "those who were run over by the street car," etc. By continually telling me these things (which I would repeat in a falsely contrite way without thinking about them) they acquired intensity over time, they acquired intensity of meaning. Before understanding what these things meant, I felt only the emotion that they evoked, dictated. Only afterward, with time, did I understand what they were saying.

Therefore, if your action derives from something dictated to you, it's child's play. If it comes from the awareness moved by the presence of a man destined for the eternal, it is no longer child's play. These years have given us a tragic example. Just think of all the people who went to the Third World for the sick, the lepers, for those with AIDS. Mother Teresa also went to the Third World for those reasons, but when they asked her, "Why do you dedicate yourself to the suffering of men?" "For the love of Jesus" she responded, leaving the journalist astonished, because Jesus is the reason why that man exists.

In any case, my answers are the expression of a mature experience that you don't yet have. This is why you have the impression of abstraction; in what I say, traces of the abstract remain in you. In continually repeating what I say, however, as time passes so does the abstraction and you begin to understand that what before seemed concrete to us was really abstract.

When we give of ourselves in the things that we are asked to do everyday, what distinguishes an act of generosity from a gesture that is truly moved?

A gesture of generosity begins with you, an impetus that originates in you. Its whole reason for being is to express something in you. The act of love arises outside you, arises from a presence that lies outside you and surrenders to the emotion or to being moved by that presence.

Generosity arises within you from an impetus that originates in you and therefore is like an escape valve. If people don't donate to the Red Cross, or the hospital, or the new bride and groom, they feel cheap – so they give. And if, instead of the 100 dollars that was asked for, they give a thousand they think they've done more. On the contrary, acting out of love originates in the exact opposite way; it arises from without, from a presence in front of you, a presence that strikes you, moves you, asks you. And you – with difficulty, perhaps with great difficulty, after many attempts to skirt the issue – finally give.

Here we see that Memores Domini represents a kind of life that is much more complex and difficult than monastic life, even though you can live the life of Memores Domini in a bourgeois or habitual fashion. Habit wears down the finish.

What an impressive distinction you have made. Saint Paul describes it in the most terrible way: I can hand my body over to be burnt and it's worth nothing if I have not charity.[45] Handing my body over to be burnt can be an impetus – like that of Jan Palch in Prague after the Russian invasion – but charity is a presence for whom I give my life, to whom I give my life. It's like the North Pole as opposed to the South Pole, things are completely up-side-down. Do you understand the vast difference in mentality between us and them? It's enough to look at those among us in certain moments to see the difference in mentality.

Many times the phrase, "Christ died for men," doesn't seem to have anything to do with me.
Because it's abstract. That Christ dies for men is an abstract expression. That Christ died for me is something so concrete that it obliges me to do everything for Him, it obliges me to understand that everything comes from Him, that He is the objective of everything I do, that He is the top of the mountain. What doesn't leave an impression on the "I" is neither mystery nor substance, it's nothing, less than nothing, it's not even ontological nothingness. During the Fraternity Retreat, I said that the "I" lies at the crossroads between the relationship with the mystery and the relationship with nothing.[46]

That Christ died for men could be an ideology. Instead, he died for me; this is a completely different story that poses the question in existential terms, not theoretical terms, existential terms. If I am to be punished, I will be punished because I didn't respond to You who died for me, not You who died for men. If I understand that He died for me, I understand that He died for my mother as well, that He died for the man I love, for the woman I love, for my son, for my friend – then I understand the rest.

If what the memory of the ages produces, sustained as it is by thousands of years, seems abstract, it's because we are empty, we are children, infants, unable to speak, infants unable to speak. There is the inability to speak which is that of the child who has nothing within and there is the inability to speak which is that of the face of the man who is filled with the greatness of his Maker. And if indeed he does speak, he stammers, because he cannot define it, like Dionysius the Areopagite said, "Who can speak of the love that Christ has for man."[47] This is what we have referred to as "too full." A three-year-old child cannot speak, because he is too empty. Surely the impression of abstraction we get from things that the ages have carried forth in minds and hearts is a symptom of emptiness, of an empty heart, of a numbed, undeveloped mind.

When you introduced the theme of hope, you explained how hope rests on faith. Can you explain how charity rests on faith?
What is faith? It's the recognition of a Presence, a Presence on which to rest everything you do, everything you are, and everything you will be. Of what is this Presence made? This is charity. Without understanding charity, we really don't understand the object of faith. Faith is the affirmation of a Presence, faith makes you take note of a Presence, it makes you affirm a Presence on which to rest your entire life – present and future (hope). But what is this Presence made of? The answer to this question is charity. Just think about how clearly this example shows that generosity is one thing and love is another. Generosity is a need of yours, a need to express yourself, while love is a need imposed upon you by a Presence, dictated by a Presence (you can't stand by). For the sake of generosity, unless you're a neurasthenic,

you'll stop at a certain point, but in front of a Presence you'll proceed even unto the point of death.

Our friend Father Zeno once made this analogy: Picture the Naviglio [the now inoperative canal that runs through the city of Milan]. The canal is a waterway with a street that runs along the side. Let's suppose that a bus pulling into the stop swerves and hits a man who was standing there waiting to board, sending him flying into the water. The people on the bus are all saying, "Look at that, the government should have done this, the government should have done that, they should have made a bigger bus stop, they should have built a bus shelter, they should have … "Everyone's putting in his two cents and in the meantime the guy is in the water is dying. When someone's life is at stake, there is no room for theories or abstraction. This particular abstraction is dictated by people's need for abstract justice. So for some there should have been a bus shelter, for others a bigger street and for others … everyone thought about what should have been done to keep the man from falling into the canal. But someone next to the door runs out, dives into the water, and saves him. A presence has no room for theories, only facts.

Do you have any idea how many people your age hear things like this? Two. You figure out the percentages.

2 Sacrifice

You would like to understand in a single flash, you would like to understand right away, you would like to understand to the point of feeling it right away. But instead, things have to be repeated and, in repeating them, it seems that they become more difficult to understand. Often it even seems that you understand less, which is a form of impatience. Because if you're forced to repeat things to understand them, either you ardently desire the truth (you have a passion for the thing you are studying), or you grumble – at a certain point you grumble: grumbling coincides with understanding less.

Yet if something is true and you keep at it and repeat it and fix your eyes on it, at a certain point it's as if, unexpectedly, the first breath of morning – the dawn – breaks, and you begin to understand. From then on, it becomes a victory, because it's like the sun after the dawn: it triumphs. Even if there are many objections, lots of darkness, many partitions that obscure the direct vision of things, the triumph of truth lies at the heart's core; you understand that the truth is there, you understand this.

Afterwards, there are also many other developments, but these are in God's hands and it's useless to describe them ahead of time. These developments can also involve a particular enjoyment in something, being moved about something, a tenderness towards the truth, so that one feels that love for Christ is not something different – it's only different in the sense that it's deeper, more gripping, than even the affection you experience with people you know ... but these developments come later.

The important thing is to begin, and this beginning is so important that God makes the first move: if you're here, it's because God began something. You're not here because *you* began but, rather, because God began something. Five years ago, ten years ago, none of you could have imagined that you would be here and you could have imagined even less that you could have persevered in staying here.

I hope all of you understand this – just as I've stated it – because it's for everyone. For me, it's even worse, at least thirteen times worse (just to use that magic number[1])! Why? Because one would like to make himself understood right away, he'd like the other to feel it right away, he'd like the other not to have to make the effort he must make; he'd like him to skip over the struggle, which is precisely the greatest aspect of affection, the affection of a mother and father. Because the ideal of affection is not between a man and a woman. Between a man and a woman, affection becomes true at the end – if they travel the path well. At its origin, affection comes forth as father and mother – the father or mother, looking at their little child, who is no bigger than the palm of their hand, would like him to walk down the road without struggling, would like him not to have to go through all the steps they went through – it pains them to know that he has to go through them.

Instead, one does what one can. Not what one can, one doesn't even do what one can, but hopefully what God lets him do, taking into account the availability of his or her freedom. Together, however, with your faithfulness if you remain, and with my faithfulness if I do what God gives me to do, then we can walk.

1 THE VALUE OF SACRIFICE

I've given this introduction because today's topic is a very important one. You can understand all the other topics humanly – faith, hope, love – but this topic, from a human standpoint, first repels and, second, seems unfair, seems like spitting up blood. A mother and father, thinking about this, would say: "How I would like to spit up blood for you!" No, the part that is reserved for each individual, that is, what God wants for you, must be done by you. But it's impossible not to collaborate, not to help, no matter what the cost.

Watershed

Today's theme seems like the least human among all the themes we've gone through but, instead, it is a *watershed*: the point where all the waters meet, where everything

meets; it is the meeting point of everything, everything …
neither faith, nor hope, nor love exist, beauty doesn't exist,
nor goodness, nor justice, nothing exists without this: it is
called sacrifice.

So sacrifice is the *watershed* of all the topics we've covered,
it's the meeting point of waters that swirl by: it becomes
an earthquake, it is clamorous and dangerous like a huge
waterfall. Sacrifice in our life is a moment as clamorous
and dangerous as a huge waterfall in which the flow of
different rivers clash.

Let's make three points and, so as not to die at number
three, not to suffocate at number three, we'll add a
corollary.

a) Sacrifice seems contrary to nature
First, sacrifice, from the natural point of view, is something
inconceivable. By nature, nothing desires sacrifice, or it
seems that nothing desires sacrifice, demands sacrifice: it
goes counter to nature. In fact, our nature is made for happiness, is made for fulfillment, is made for beauty, is made
for truth. Nature is made for happiness and sacrifice goes
against this; and therefore – let's say – at the very least it is
incomprehensible. Sacrifice from the natural point of view
is incomprehensible, and if one gets a little irritated, it
becomes even intolerable, because it's something that goes
against what we're made for: it seems like an injustice. For
this reason Pavese, in his diary, when he was still a boy, at
seventeen years old, wrote that sacrifice is something inconceivable, "unbelievable" he says.[2]

b) When it became interesting

When did sacrifice start to become something of value? Value is what is worth the trouble. The word value is what relates the ephemeral – ephemeral time, the ephemeral circumstance – to its destiny, and therefore it's no longer ephemeral, no longer fleeting: it is *worth the trouble*. Value means that it's worth the trouble – what doesn't pass away, what isn't useless, is worth the trouble. Therefore value is what remains, that is, what connects you with your destiny, because the word destiny is the one that dominates anywhere and everywhere – for each hair on your head, for each fibre of your heart.

When does sacrifice become not something intolerable, in comprehensible, "unbelievable," but something of value? When, according to you?

When it is an act of love.

Great, that's a beautiful bouquet of words!

When it is a free act.

A punch that splits open your eye is also a free act!

When it has a goal.

When it is done for another.

Okay, we're getting closer: "When it is done for another," which is not a reason, because "another" vanishes like the dry autumn leaves. The leaves vanish, even beautiful flowers vanish, and the other person vanishes: if you go to see him five days later in the coffin, you run away, for various reasons. "Done for another" has a goal, it can be something good, but sad; a good thing that is sad. When I pass by the military cemetery and see the tens of thousands of dead soldiers, dead "for the fatherland," there was a goal; even if it wasn't wanted, there was a goal. However, deep, deep down, it's a goal that would make one strangle those who caused their death.

It's worth the trouble when the sacrifice is done for something else that doesn't wither like the autumn leaves, that doesn't rot like a man who dies; something else that challenges time, something else that grows more beautiful with time, that persists, and that makes even you persist in the same way; otherwise it's something "unbelievable" or, using a less juvenile word, sad, but sad in the ugly sense of the term: bitter.

So, don't you have anything else to say? These are the biggest things in life, and people go to the bar here out in front to drink a glass of wine and this is their satisfaction for the day, or they walk together arm-in-arm through the countryside and that, for one or two hours, is everything. Everything is swept away by a terrible wind that nullifies everything, makes it nothing; a wind so strong, so all-conquering that it nullifies everything.

The word sacrifice began, historically, to become a great word from the time that God became a man, was born of a young woman, was small, walked with little steps, then began to speak (He spoke in Hebrew), and then began to help His father, who was a carpenter; then He grew older and began to leave the house without His mother understanding why. He said: "I'm going" and she said, "Go." She didn't know why. Then she heard them shouting in the town square; many shouted out against Him because He spoke, and some cried and many others, instead, were full of anger against Him; then He came home and was sad and his mother didn't even dare to say: "Why? How come? What did you say?" It's possible that sometimes she asked Him, but she understood that it was useless to ask Him, because even she wouldn't have understood.

From the time that God became a man; and then, later, He began to speak to the people; and the people seemed to follow Him when He performed strange deeds (or miracles), but the day after they forgot – He was there alone – and therefore the number of those against Him grew, until they took Him and killed Him. From the time that man was killed, nailed to a cross, and shouted: "Father, why have you abandoned me?" – which is the most human cry of desperation ever heard on the earth – and then said: "Forgive them because they do not know what they are doing," and then shouted: "Into your hands I commend my spirit." From that moment, when that man was stretched out and nailed to the cross, from that moment the word sacrifice became the centre, not of that man's life, but of the life of "every" man, and the destiny of every man depends on that death. The word sacrifice became, therefore, the centre of history, so much so that we even calculate the years from when He was born: "before" or "after." The years of history are numbered like that: not that it's essential, but it's significant.

From the moment that man died on the cross, the word sacrifice became a huge word, a great word, and it revealed – as when the sun rises, like a sun that rises – that the whole life of every man is woven of sacrifices, is full of shudders of sacrifice, is, as it were, dominated by the need to sacrifice:

a mother to generate a child; a father to take care of the mother and the child; each of us to be a true friend to another person, to continue the path with someone you love, to go to work and earn your monthly paycheck, to go to see on Mont Blanc one of the most beautiful spectacles you can see, to climb it. In short, sacrifice here, sacrifice there – to pay attention for an hour now, to speak to you for an hour now … it's impossible to avoid sacrifice, and over everything looms the greatest sacrifice you can conceive of, which is death.

The word sacrifice is a repugnant word, so much so that the Greeks, whose highest form of worship was the cult of the beauty of the body (not believing in anything, the only beautiful thing there is in this world, worthy of veneration and admiration, is the beauty of the body), they who only believed in the beauty of the body the word they never pronounced, except with hatred, the word that referred to the gods – these strange powers – as the source of death. Death was the worst thing you could conceive of and there was nothing you could do about it.

Sacrifice was inconceivable, repulsive, yet at a certain point in history sacrifice started to become interesting, or had to do with man's interests, that is, man's destiny: when Christ died on the cross, so that men could be saved from death, that is, so that things could be saved from corruption, from becoming worms, small and numerous. From that moment the word sacrifice became interesting; holding onto everything we've hinted at before, man understood that no part of his life could avoid sacrifice.

In dying, Jesus not only made us understand that sacrifice was interesting, interesting for the destiny of man – He died so that men could reach their destiny and save themselves from death, through death – but also revealed, made us see, that it was not something strange, that it was something interesting but not strange, because all of life is like that. If you look at all of your life, all of your life is made of sacrifices, from the moment when you have to get up in the morning.

The cross of Christ revealed, on the one hand, the dominion that sacrifice has on the life of all and, on the other hand, that its meaning was not necessarily negative, or better, that it had a mysteriously positive significance: it was the condition for men to reach their destiny. "Through your cross you have redeemed the world," through your cross, O Christ, you have saved the world.

c) When it becomes a value for the life of man
Here is a step to take: in us – in me, in you – when does sacrifice become a value? Come on, answer me, because it is not the same logic as before. Before, I said that sacrifice acquired value when Christ died. But He died.

Sacrifice becomes a moral value, that is, a value for the life of man, when it becomes a correspondence, i.e., co-responsibility, a response to Christ's death, in order to save one's own life and the lives of men; when it becomes an acceptance that the only way to reach destiny, to conquer death, is to mount the cross of Christ (even us): participating in Christ's death. Co-responsibility, conscious responsibility, a conscious response to Christ's death: "You, Christ, die for me. I adhere to you in your death." How? Through the sacrifices you have me make. "My life accepts the sacrifices you have me carry out as my bond to your death." For this reason it is also called offering: offering your own life to Christ, as a participation in His death. So, even my sacrifice of getting up in the morning, of tolerating my father, my mother, my wife, my husband, the kids ... even that becomes good.

On Good Friday, we sing the hymn of the cross, *Crux fidelis inter omnes*, faithful cross, true tree among trees, tree that doesn't die. So Jesus's sacrifice – which is the great value that saves the world from all its misery and from death – becomes our value if we participate in it, if we accept from Christ the method He establishes for making us participate in His sacrifice. For example, He sends me an illness, He makes me be treated unfairly, He disappoints me in love, He makes me sacrifice an affection.

Sacrifice becomes a moral value for man, when man, through it, participates in the initiative God takes to liberate us from death and from evil. What is the initiative God takes to save us from death and from evil? The death of Christ. However, think how God became a man and was assassinated to give back the possibility of happiness to those who assassinated Him!

If the sacrifice is accepting the circumstances of life, as they happen, because they make us correspondent, participants in the death of Christ, then sacrifice becomes the keystone of all life – life's value is in the sacrifice one lives – but also the keystone for understanding the history of man. The entire history of man depends on that man dead on the cross, and I can influence the history of man – I can influence the people who live in Japan now, the people in danger at sea now; I can intervene to help the pain of the women who lose their children now, in this moment – if I accept the sacrifice that this moment imposes.

Because of original sin

Why, then, is sacrifice that law of the dynamic of life – why does the dynamism of life have sacrifice as its deepest law, why does it have happiness as a goal and have sacrifice as a conditioning law; to pass exams you must struggle – struggle or sacrifice is the same – why? Is it right that God became man and died on the cross just to reveal to all men that life's sacrifices are the condition for life to grow, for life to be true? Why is it that way?

First, you can't tell God: "You're wrong!" What man can say to God: "You're wrong!"?

All this is true: Christ died on the cross for the salvation of men, and each of us can collaborate in the salvation of the world by accepting the sacrifice of the circumstances through which we're made to pass. Because the existence of the individual and the history of everyone have an enormous weight at their origin, a gigantic, tragic, mountain that weighs down and blocks everything. Man's nature is tragic because of this terrible beginning that is called original sin, which is a fact that we cannot explain, yet without this mysterious phenomenon nothing is explained any longer. Sacrifice is no longer explained, but nothing would be explained any longer. There are those more fortunate and those less fortunate; this is certainly an intolerable injustice: one is fortunate and the other not fortunate, why?

Original sin: read, in the Letter to the Romans, chapter seven.

2 WHAT SACRIFICE CONSISTS OF

Second step. The aim of the first step is to show above all the incomprehensibility of sacrifice, because it seems to be against nature. It begins to become meaningful when God dies on the cross. And this begins to reveal not only that the word sacrifice has a meaning but also that everything, all of our life, and all of our days, are full of an infinite number of sacrifices, small or great. If one accepts these sacrifices to conform to the death of Christ, to collaborate in the death of Christ to save the world, then one who makes a sacrifice here, now, perhaps helps, without realizing it, a poor mother who in Yugoslavia is losing her child to a grenade: there is neither time nor space. For the things beyond time and space – like the value of sacrifice, Christ's or ours – there is no time or space, time and space have no limit. The sacrifice I make for the love of Christ, now, can help a person or so many other persons who are shipwrecked in the Gulf of Tonkin now, who knows?

Let's see now, second, what sacrifice consists of. What is sacrifice made of? It is not made of death on the cross, because it is also a sacrifice for me to be here, worn out, speaking now (in a manner of speaking; no, not in a manner of speaking), it is a sacrifice for you to be here listening to me; it is a sacrifice to take the little book in hand and say "Lord, make haste to help me." It isn't a sacrifice just because we are revoltingly distracted, but if we were to consider and think about what we're saying ... Let's realize, then, what this "monster" that is sacrifice consists of.

The Bible – *The Religious Sense*[3] says – has a precise word to indicate something man adores as God, while it isn't God: it's called an idol. To affirm or look for the truth where it isn't, to affirm or look for idolatry, in short, is falsehood, is a lie. What we call sin is falsehood; it is sin because it is falsehood: it is not true! And the psalm says, very acutely: "Look at the characteristics of the idol: it has eyes but cannot see; ears but cannot hear; a mouth but cannot speak."[4] What does this mean? It doesn't keep the promises for which it seems to be made. What doesn't keep promises is falsehood. My God, how sad the majority of weddings are, when I have to do them: the majority of weddings are a sadness without end because, except for a line that God sustains, they are false promises.

Sacrifice is to go against falsehood. Going against falsehood, doing something in a true, loyal, sincere, just way: this is sacrifice. To do what is true, a sacrifice is needed: you must tear yourself away from falsehood, you must tear falsehood away, you must resist the current, or better still, the landslide of falsehood. You must be there and let all the debris pass.

Without sacrifice there can be no truth in a relationship. Keep this in mind: these are the sentences that define all of life, that are important for all of life, because they are invincible. No Donadoni can defeat them – in my day it was Meazza![5] No atomic bomb can destroy them. Without sacrifice there is no truth in a relationship.

Try to think of when you are affectively attached to a person: it's lie upon lie, if it isn't continually controlled by sacrifice. Without sacrifice there is no true relationship, which means that the other – any object or person – is not valued according to its nature (in fact, the meaning of nature can even be inverted); it is affirmed by your liking, by your instinct, because you want to snatch it in the way that a miser snatches money. What a lie! "Because it is *nice*": I think that's the most normal adjective for a lie – a pretext, finally.

We identify affirming something with snatching it. Affirming something is love, it is affirming the other; snatching it means bending it in your direction, making it a slave.

Therefore sacrifice does not mean suspending the will for something, suspending love for someone or something; it does not mean to eliminate anything, but to rein in the will that is behaving against the nature of the thing.

If you can't use the thing according to its destiny, if you can't use this affective relationship according to its destiny, you're a criminal, it's a crime! "But, sacrifice is impossible!" Sacrifice is necessary just as not committing a crime is necessary.

Sacrifice is not to suspend the will for something, but to rein in the will that is not according to the nature of the thing. For this reason all premarital relations are wrong, all of them; they impose twisted paths that are never straightened out; and they affirm a selfishness – "what feels good" as the ultimate criterion of the relationship – that never redeems itself. Read pages 453 and 454 in *Un avvenimento di vita cioè una storia.*[6]

3   THE TRUEST SACRIFICE IS RECOGNIZING A PRESENCE

Third step. What is the truest sacrifice? What is the sacrifice that is most united to truth? What is the sacrifice that is farthest from error, from evil, from falsehood? What is the sacrifice that is most united to truth?

It is here that one understands that everything is connected. The answer to this is the point at which one understands that sacrifice is identical to the drama and grandeur of love.

The truest sacrifice is to recognize a presence.

I understand extremely well that you don't understand anything, yet if you never understand anything, what a miserable life! You will understand. Be patient, you'll understand!

The truest sacrifice is to recognize a presence. What does it mean to recognize a presence? The I, instead of affirming itself, affirms you. This is the greatest devotion: "There is no greater love than to lay down one's life for one's friends"[7]; it is the same as giving one's life. To affirm you in order to affirm the I, to make the I live, to affirm you as the goal of the I's action, to affirm you is love for you. For this reason it is really a sacrifice of oneself: not of a finger, not of one's hair, not of the outcome of the school year … No, no, no, no! It is the total sacrifice of the self:

to affirm the other implies the forgetting of ourselves, which is the opposite of being attached to ourselves; we sacrifice to the other.

The truest sacrifice is to recognize a presence, which means the truest sacrifice is to love.

Sadness and asking

What is the true feeling that sacrifice affirms as the strongest feeling in life? Sacrifice affirms sadness as the strongest, gravest, and greatest feeling of life, because I cannot succeed in affirming the presence that I want to affirm. I love a person, I would like to affirm her with all of my self and I am not able: she dies, two days later, she dies. You are not able to affirm the object of love – the presence is the proper object of love – fully, adequately: therefore human relationships cannot avoid being sadness.

It is such sadness in the face of the unfulfilled presence that unleashes the appeal, the last appeal of the Bible. "Come, Lord Jesus,"[8] come, because You who died on the cross, only You can make the person I love happy – can be destiny fulfilled – and in this way make me happy, as a consequence!

I will tell you an impressive fact from my life. A guy and a girl, very bright, very young, were engaged, in one of the towns of Abruzzi; they were supposed to be married in a few months. A certain Father Semini, a Verona Father, went there to do a week of appeal for the missions. One night, while they were going home, the guy says to the girl: "Listen, if I don't sacrifice myself and become a missionary – there are so many people who live without knowing God, unhappy – if I didn't sacrifice myself, I wouldn't feel worthy of you, I would be ashamed before you, I would be ashamed to tell you: 'I love you'." And she: "sighs, cry, and other woe resounded through the air without stars."[9] But the conclusion was impressive: he became a missionary and she, after a few months, entered a convent to become a missionary sister. And now both are missionaries: he in a missionary post and she a missionary sister. By the way, the families are still fighting amongst themselves because they broke off the engagement!

This seldom happens in life, but it is the ideal made real: the ideal that one thinks about truly becomes real, because in such a sacrifice what I said about the *Sevillanas* happens. Human destiny is that as a friend goes away, the ship becomes ever smaller, smaller, until it disappears over the horizon. Instead, the opposite happens here: a small point on the horizon becomes ever larger, larger and larger and closer and closer.

4 THE SACRIFICE OF FAITH AND THE CHARISM

Corollary. Read John's gospel, the entire first chapter: the first half is the supreme theory; the second half is the most impressive fact that can be told, that of Andrew and John. I was happy when, at the end of the last exercises of the Fraternity, where one hundred and fifty Spanish workers were present, Carmen called me from Madrid that night and said: "Here everyone is speaking about John and Andrew, Andrew and John, Andrew and John!" And in fact that time I had insisted on it for almost half an hour.

How – pay attention to the problem! – how is this presence of Christ recognizable, lovable, to the point of sacrifice (this is faith as sacrifice, it is the sacrifice of faith) for me? Why are we together, my friend? We are here because Christ is among us; Christ, after two thousand years, has put you here, with me whom you did not know, and we are together because of this; we don't know how, but we are together because of this, and all the many reasons that we have for being here don't exhaust it … they don't give even a small hint of the solution to this question: "How do we manage to be here? How does Christ manage to be here, among us?" While the love that each of us has for the other, the interest that each has for the destiny of the other, is because of *Christ who is among us*, it is through Christ who is among us, it is an affirmation of Christ who is among us.

We know Christ is here for so many reasons that could not be explained, if I didn't understand the hypothesis of the great possibility that among us there is something other that is greater than us. It is inconceivable, in the whole world it is inconceivable, that there be a group of people who on Saturday afternoon get together as we do. There is something greater than us among us. And recognizing something greater than the self, something that reason isn't able to identify well in all its reasons, but that it cannot reject without risking the greatest irrationality it can risk, is faith: "I believe, Lord."

Christ remains present with us: "I will be with you always, until the end of the world"; for this reason I know Maria, Genoveffa, and Silvia, for this reason I know all those I know and I know all those I don't know. Christ remains present with us, every day until the end of the world, within the historical circumstances that the mystery of the Father establishes, the historical circumstances through which the mystery of the Father makes you recognize and love the Presence of something other, of Christ. These historical circumstances, through which the Father makes us understand the presence of another Presence, the presence of something other that is greater, belong to what is called *charism*: the historical circumstances that create our Movement or the Gruppo Adulto.

Charism means grace, a gift, the gift that the Infinite makes of Himself, and it indicates the existential form of temperament, of mentality, of environment by which this gift assumes certain physical traits for you, assumes an accent, a particular way of looking at things. In Asia they can be large, narrow, small, tall and short, full of colds, with smothered voices, with ugly or beautiful faces ... you can say "it doesn't matter," and one can love anyone forever, and that's what really happens! In this way, for example, some of our people go to Kampala, amidst the rhinoceros and crocodiles, or amidst those ill with AIDS, whom our friend Rose takes care of as if they were brothers and sisters, because of which she is well known in almost half of Kampala.

He who has been reached by a charism can no longer follow Christ if he abandons the charism. It would be a betrayal. All the people who told me: "The Movement has all these defects, I'm leaving," all those who left, lost everything, understood nothing any longer, so much so that at a certain point they return. One of you, if you were to go away, would no longer understand anything; if you are called through these circumstances, through these circumstances you will reach your happiness, you will help men and women, you will love people and you will love Christ. If Christ brought you to know Him through these circumstances, represented by these faces, it is through these faces, these circumstances that He changes you, that He makes your heart, your soul, your mind great.

"If they could touch Jesus up close!" said the Pope three weeks ago – "Touch, but where? See, where? If they see Him in you they will say: 'My Lord and my God' like Saint Thomas."[10] In you: Christ is present in our midst, one touches Christ through us, one sees Christ through us. Whereas if we abandon Him we don't see anything! "If you continue, you will see greater things than this," Jesus said, "and much greater."[11] I always think of these words of Jesus as I remember my beginnings as a priest and how I began to teach the hour of religion at the Berchet high school: three or four teenagers followed me; my furthest thought was of enlarging the group. Now I get a quiver of fear when I think of it!

"He who remains in me, he who will be faithful in belonging to me [and you belong to me through the unity among you, the companionship among you, because I am present there] will do the things that I do and even greater good than this."[12]

"Touch where? See where? If they will see Him in you, they will say 'My Lord and my God'."

Sacrifice seems like death – mortification – and it is the principle of life, the principle of true life, that conquers time and space, that does not give in to falsehood. There is no experience of sacrifice that doesn't make us greater, if accepted: "He is, if He changes."[13]

To understand these things one must be graced, one needs God to help him. God, only God, can make us understand being as it is, and sacrifice is the fundamental condition of being in time and in space.

Thank goodness that outside of time and space, my friends, there is pure enjoyment: "to glory in a kingdom/... fulfills the longing of every heart."[14] It is paradise that fulfills all the images of a feast that the heart desires. For this reason, at the exercises in Rimini,[15] I said that the human I, that is, the human heart, is the crossroads in the relationship between the eternal (the infinite) and nothingness: there is no alternative. The difficulty, the extremely great difficulty – that must be lived in fear and trembling – in imagining the infinite is understandable, but nothingness is not understandable.

In *The Religious Sense*, where does it say this? It is the most beautiful page:[16] the poem by Montale.[17] It is useless for him to say that, when he turns around, he perceives nothingness, that is, things are not, they die, they vanish; one cannot say "so everything is nothing," because things are there. If they are there, even for only an instant, one cannot say, one cannot decide, "Everything is nothing." To say that everything is nothing is a metaphor, a desperate one.

"I'm tired of suffering, Lord; give me life according to Your word."[18] How can you read a sentence like this every week without learning anything? "I'm tired of suffering" – everyone can see himself in this, right? Everyone is tired out, in the evening everyone is tired out, at noon everyone is tired out, at three o'clock everyone is tired out. So "Let's suffer no longer!" No, not to suffer anymore means not to live anymore, in that you'd have to be dead not to suffer. Suffering is inevitable. As if I were to say: "You need to eat in order to live." It's something evident!

We're always tired of suffering because suffering is not in the nature of man's destiny, it's not "according to His word"; according to His word man isn't made for unhappiness, as a passage of the book of Wisdom says: "God made man for happiness."[19] When you say a sentence like this, I'd like to know, what do you think? Faced with this contradiction, how do you respond? "We're tired of suffering": rightly so, because suffering isn't according to man's destiny. "According to Your word" means according to the destiny that You gave man. Rather, "Give me life" is according to His word – make me live. What's the misconception? Pitting "suffering" and "life" against each other, whereas suffering is a condition of life – and the more one suffers and is capable of suffering, the fuller one's life is. The best example of this is one that everyone knows, even if they never think about it: it's Jesus, who suffered more than anyone, because He gave his life for everything.

"I'm tired of suffering," therefore, make me understand the reason and love that exist in suffering, make me understand the humanity that exists in suffering, make me understand the love toward Being that lies in suffering, make me understand the love toward Christ that lies in suffering, make me understand the love toward You, O Mystery, that lies in suffering. Then, one is no longer scandalized by suffering. "I'm tired of suffering" is the scandal of suffering that seems to be the opposite of "Give me life." Instead, it's the condition for life.

"According to Your word," then, changes meaning: according to your plan (word), sacrifice becomes the moving force of life. In what way does sacrifice become the moving force of life, as it was for Jesus? Why did Jesus suffer? "No one can lay a foundation other than the one that is already found in Jesus."[20] As it was for Jesus, our life can be neither intense nor useful – neither alive for us nor useful for others – if it doesn't imitate Jesus. At the base of our life lies Christ's pain – as does Christ's glory, so does Christ's pain: "As you have freely received, freely give."[21] So you can understand that prayer: "So that through the experience of the Spirit we may serve the human community and build Your Kingdom."[22] The building up of the Kingdom: to make the world the Kingdom of Christ, to make the world an edifice of Christ, life needs to be born out of sacrifice; sacrifice is the manure, the fertilizer – like my poor mother, who, when we were walking in the fields on vacation, made this observation daily: "What a mystery this is! How does bread, food, grow? On the soil where manure is placed." It wasn't a banal comparison, it was an observation that none of us makes – the manure is sacrifice, life that no longer seems to be life.

You have said that the sentiment that sacrifice affirms as the truest is sadness. Going back through the lesson, this was the part that I had most difficulty understanding, because I was asking myself, so then, as one continues to go on, does he becomes sadder? Then I thought back to the relationships with my friends and this is what I understood: if I'm in a relationship with my friends, looking to tell them what happiness is for them, I'm doubly wrong, because on the one hand, I'm not capable of saying what happiness is for my friends. On the other hand, I'm violent because it's as if I were trying to take away their freedom to stand in front of what they have.
Very correct.

So as I see it, sadness is saying: "Lord, I'm not capable, accomplish what I'm not able to do"; and this sadness is good, because it places me anew in a relationship with the other; the relationship with the other starts up again in another way.
Sadness is an inevitable and significant characteristic of life, because in life, in its every moment – above all, the more intense the moment is – you have the perception of something that is still lacking; sadness is an absence that causes one to suffer.

What makes sadness into something good? Recognizing it as a meaningful tool in God's plan. God's plan implies this: that life is always, in any situation – and even more so when life is more committed – subject to the perception of something that's missing. And this is providential for making us understand that, as Pär Lagerkvist said, there's no one who responds to the voice that cries out in the world's emptiness. But why is there the voice, why is there the cry?[23] The fact that life is sad is the most compelling occasion for making us understand that our destiny is something greater, it's the greater mystery. And when this mystery comes to us, by becoming man, this becomes a hundred times more compelling. It doesn't take away the sadness, because the way God becomes man is such that you have Him without having Him, you already have Him and you don't have Him yet. It seems like this to us because we don't see Him – I don't see Him as I see you – I know that He is here, because you're here, because we're here. But even for the first disciples it was this way: for the first disciples, Christ was an ordinary man, a man like all others. Sadness is the condition that God has placed at the core of human existence so that man never calmly deludes himself into thinking that what he has can be enough for him.

This is how I explained this theme. Everything else, like the thoughts that you had, are correct, but the true reason for the link between sadness and life is that sadness is an integral part *not* of the nature of man's destiny, but of man's existence, that is, of the journey towards destiny – and it is present every step of the way. The more you love this step, the more this step is beautiful for you, the more it's enchanting for you, the more it's yours, the more you'll understand that you're missing the thing that you're waiting for most.

Last year, you said: if one doesn't feel the fear of sacrifice, so that Christ is his only shelter of hope, what kind of man is he? This struck me, because, when speaking with people, the fear of sacrifice never came up. So I asked myself if this was because we're so abstract that we live a little far from reality?

That's very correct. What you've already eliminated in terms of your will to accept, in terms of your capacity to evaluate what is good, in terms of your judgment of pertinence, appears abstract to you. If I ask you: "Is what I say right or not?" – "right or not" meaning "does it have a reason to it or doesn't it?" – and you answer: "Yes, it has a reason, but it's abstract," this shows the fraud in you. If there is a reason, you can't say: "but it's abstract," because reason is what responds to the need of the heart, it's what corresponds to the person's destiny. I gave this answer once, and everyone remained skeptical – and rightly so! – because it's the condemnation of your superficiality. To consider as abstract a value whose reason you see, which gives you no reason to go against it, to consider it abstract because you can't touch it as you can your hair, you can't touch it as you touch the tip of your nose, you can't touch it as you caress a face, means being dishonest, because it's a denial of the link with one's own heart, with the sense of one's own destiny that the thing reveals. Because reason is the revelation of the relationship of something with its own destiny, reason is what is in relationship with our heart, with the needs of our heart and, therefore, with our destiny.

We mustn't be afraid of sacrifice. We must be afraid of what is abstract; the abstract is the condemnation of our human dignity. The abstract is what eludes your connection with destiny. Therefore the abstract is what eludes what your heart is made for, and it tends to identify what is concrete with the tip of your nose that you touch, with the hair that you put in place, with your stomach that aches, with the ice cream that you like – and all this is so ironically concrete that it ends up rotting in the tomb.

So, then, abstraction is a distraction?
Yes, the abstract is a willed distraction. For that reason I spoke of fraud; it's a distraction from reason; that is, from your nature, which is the need for a destiny that begins to make itself visible in reason.

Speaking of sadness, you told us to read the passage in the book published by the magazine Il Sabato where it says that "you don't need to be afraid of sacrifice because it is the condition for the permanence of tenderness and gladness.[24] I wasn't really able to understand the link between sadness and gladness.
The permanence of tenderness and therefore of the gladness that springs from it – tenderness is the first glimmer of possessing, the morning glimmer or the evening glimmer – the permanence of tenderness hinges on it being true tenderness. It must really be true tenderness to hold out, to last. To be true tenderness, it must love the object truly and the object must be perceived for what it truly is. How can you have tenderness towards a being who gives you life as your mother does, who then abandons you (because at a certain point, she dies)? This is tenderness that today, if you think about it, is already (starting from today) drowning in a pool of sadness. You care a lot for a particular person, but how

can you care a lot for that person, how can you feel tenderness towards her, while thinking that tomorrow you may not see her anymore, that tomorrow she'll die, or that tomorrow she'll go to Kamchatka, which is way over in eastern Russia? What would you do? Only if you perceive the eternity of the companionship with this person, only if you perceive that the relationship with this person, what she brings out in you, is the sign of your relationship with the eternal, only then is the relationship with this person an eternal relationship. Love for this person is eternal love.

It is sacrifice in the present that permits the permanence of tenderness. If you have tenderness for a person and you think that you can lose this person tomorrow – because what's the difference between a husband who leaves his wife and a mother who dies before you do? – the tenderness remains in words only, it's sad. Instead, if you accept this as a condition for the journey, both you and your mother are destined for a happy destination, both taking different voyages, but ones that are equally painful, difficult, full of work, full of sacrifice. If you accept this sacrifice, if you accept that the trip will be tough, if you accept that the distance to cover will be a struggle, if you accept this, it allows you to have this tenderness, it allows the evidence of love that lasts; you won't be overwhelmed by any circumstance. But is it so difficult to understand these things? These things are difficult to understand in two cases: either you have never loved anyone in particular, or you stopped loving someone (or you loved in such a way that the love had to end; that is, it wasn't true caring for someone: you can't think of an "I'll love you for twenty-three years."

Because of this, divorce is the ghastly reduction of love between man and woman: "I love you desperately, intensely, for as long as I want – that is, for three years." Great!).

Last time, you said that sacrifice becomes a moral value when it becomes a correspondence, that is, co-responsibility – a response to the death of Christ. So I want to ask: could it also not become a response of freedom?

If, in sacrifice, with sacrifice, freedom doesn't become connection with or companionship with Christ, a response to Christ who calls, there's nothing more stupid and beastly, as Pavese said, than sacrifice. On the other hand, if you adopt a system of avoiding sacrifice at all costs, you have to come to a halt in the puddle that you're in, because as soon as you move the bow, you find a rock ahead – sacrifice means changing course.

In other words, sacrifice, first, is a waste of time, a bringing to fruition things that are incomplete; and second, it's truly beastly, as Pavese said. An animal, a beast, is something without reason. .

When does accepting and embracing a sacrifice become reasonable? When it is accepted, because it's in the plan that God has for your life, it is part of the plan that God has for your life. The plan God has for your life is called Christ: it's part of the company of Christ. Following Christ, you adhere to His companionship by accepting the sacrifices that the companionship imposes. And with His sacrifice, Christ saves the world: you have something to do with saving the world. So what does it mean, then, when your father and mother, or better yet, one of your friends, knowing that you're on this path, asks you: "Listen, go and say a Hail Mary for me too"? It means that he recognizes, *bon gré, mal gré*, that you have something to do with his journey toward destiny, with his happiness, you have something to do with his happiness that is different from how he wanted you; different, meaning that "you truly have something to do with it."

Why do you speak of charism in the lesson on sacrifice?
If, historically speaking, life is a charism – that is, the gift of the Spirit, which is participation in the mystery of Being, participation in the soul that creates the cosmos, participation in the happiness of each individual man as history's supreme destiny – inasmuch as it implies a sacrifice (cross), it implies a sacrifice only to the extent that it is requested by the charism itself: that is, the work of the Spirit is a dramatic plan, and sacrifice is an inevitable part of this drama.

What is a charism? Charism is a word that comes from Greek, meaning "gift." And the gift is the communication of the Being, of the mystery of Being, to our life. For this reason, the charism is given by the Holy Spirit, *donum Dei Altissimi.* The Holy Spirit communicates itself to Anna's life through a set of circumstances. Because of this, the Holy Spirit is always original, because it doesn't follow our logic, but leads to a consequence that is one hundred thousand times more beautiful than our logic. The Holy Spirit communicates itself to Mr Luca's life, communicates itself to Mr Guido's life, the Holy Spirit communicates Being as Anna's life, as Guido's life, as my life, in ways that are different from each other. The Spirit doesn't make one face the same as another – our faces are all born from the gift of creation. This gesture of creation creates faces that are all different, not one is identical to another – it doesn't make one "I" identical to another (a self-consciousness the same as another). Through what did God make me and make you? Through different circumstances of which the father and mother are manifestations; they are the aspect that is most plainly evident. In different circumstances, He creates Cecca; in different circumstances He created me, so that out of all this diversity, the great poem of His creation would be composed.

What is called charism are those circumstances through which the Spirit communicates the awareness of Christ to me and you in such a way that He allows you and me to know Him in a particular way; He allows this other person and that other person to know Him in a true way, but through a different method. The charism is the method through which the Spirit – through circumstances of life, of temperament, of education, of companionship, of concrete suggestions, of concrete discoveries – lets you and me know what Christ is. Therefore if Christ is everything in our life, nothing binds us together more than the charism, because it's the most important thing there is: through the charism, you can recognize yourself; through the charism, I recognize myself; through the charism I recognize who you are. The charism represents the first space where the Mystery of God becomes a gift for man, a space impacted by Christ, characterized by particular circumstances that constitute the I, that make up the context in which the I lives, always creating a companionship, that is, a piece of the Church: the Church is made up of many pieces, which are many charisms.

But then, since you have to act in line with Christian doctrine, with the awareness of Christ, you can't say: "I'll make it up myself, I'll choose whom I want," no! "I'll choose that priest because he's handsome, athletic, speaks well and also has gel in his hair, or because he has a nice voice." You can't say that. You can be assigned, by the Spirit, to a situation and circumstances in which it's not possible for you to gladden or lighten the weight of your journey through a companionship that is more beautiful and easier, more lucid and transparent; but it can be through the companionship of a slovenly and old pastor, with a raspy voice, with people who are boorish and distracted in church – that can be the path He assigns to you.

So, if everything derives from the modality with which the Spirit forms your features, your life, your journey through circumstances, you must conform to those circumstances. And conforming to those circumstances is a sacrifice; it's renouncing your own circumstances. So a person who has encountered CL can't be a good Christian if he forgets this; theoretically, one is free to go where one wants, but objectively, existentially, historically, if one doesn't comply, obey, doesn't take into consideration, doesn't allow himself to be enlightened by the way in which God struck him, by the circumstances of a certain encounter, if he doesn't adhere to this, he won't ever seriously be a Christian, he won't ever be happy, he won't ever reach a position to be useful to others. More simply:

he'll always be unhappy because that's a betrayal. In the army, they give you a flame thrower, because you're in the flame-throwing company, and you say: "A flame thrower for me? Don't even think about it! I'll take a dagger." And in the flame-throwing company, you go forward with your dagger; you get burned before the others! If you're assigned to the flame-throwing company, then throw flames!

Why, then, is sacrifice inherent to every charism? Because a charism is a set of circumstances that you don't establish, and you must follow them and recognize their importance. If a flower springs up with really long and narrow sepals, it becomes a magnificent and dazzling corolla if it follows its nature. It doesn't say: "I want to have small sepals with a whatchamacallit on the outside!" You must follow circumstances that you don't establish. If you knew ... when you discover this, you'll understand! You can't love a person, a man can't love a woman, without passing through these conditions. He can't. If he wants to love the woman the way he wants he destroys or loses her, which is the same thing. Losing her is healthier, because at least he realizes it! You can destroy without realizing it.

What does it mean that the truest sacrifice is to recognize a
presence: instead of affirming myself, I affirm you, love you?
What does it mean that the truest sacrifice is to love?
The big issue is this: the phenomenon of sacrifice reaches its highest point of intensity, of wound, of weight, but also of usefulness for the world, in the recognition of a presence.

I'll give two examples – I don't think you can find three! – that I believe can explain everything.

When a boy loves a girl – it's useless. The comparisons that you make all lead back to the relationship between child and parents or man and woman, because those are the two basic images that reflect the mystery of the Trinity on man's life, on the life of creation – if a man loves a woman, either he doesn't reflect on it (then, poor guy, he only enjoys one per cent of things, he reduces things; all men are busy reducing things to the point of losing their souls, not enlarging things, not making them greater, no, but rather reducing, making smaller, to consume more, thinking that they're possessing more) or else, if he reflects on it, he understands that everything that he does (whether at home or in relationships), he is forced to do – forced to act according to the temperament and the will of the person he loves. He's forced to do everything as another wants. If he thinks that there's no sacrifice, it's because his face is covered as if with gauze, obscured by a fleeting pleasure, by a fleeting taste, by the fleeting taste of tenderness that isn't self-aware, that isn't aware of its own roots, its motives, its destinies. Do you think that one can love another person while doing what one feels like? Do you think so? No! So then what? Then there's no source of sacrifice greater than recognizing a presence.

But this is simply the foreshadowing – the natural, human foreshadowing, a foreshadowing, and therefore ephemeral – of the big question of the mystery of God and the mystery of Christ. Why was there this great man, Christ? "I always do what my Father wills,"[25] "what my

Father wills I always do," "as my Father is at work, so am I at work as well,"[26] "I follow the will of my Father,"[27] "made obedient even unto death."[28] Enter into the consciousness of Christ, a man just as Mario is a man and I am a man, a man like us! He is a man! The greatness of the man-Christ is that He lived recognizing that the value of every thing lies in the will of Another, "of the Father who is with me,"[29] "my Father is always with me," "Father, until now I have glorified you, now the hour has come: glorify your Son"[30] (but this is the sign of the end of time). The phrase "to glorify the other" is beautiful: it means that the other is the criterion of my action. If the criterion of my acting is the other, I must sacrifice what I think and like: "Father, if it is possible may I not die, but not my will, but yours be done."[31] This is the instant in which, even if ever so subtly perceived, the great pain that Christ chose and embraced seems to prevail. For Christ, recognizing the mystery of the Father constituted the most difficult source of pain, of self-sacrifice in His life. Just think, He came to save the world – "I have come to light a fire on the earth, what do I want, what can I want, if not that it thrive everywhere?'[32] And yet the Father commanded Him to stay among the Jews. A few kilometres away were cities like Tyre with large pagan populations that would have received Him a hundred times better.

He didn't go there. In fact, He said to that woman who touched His cloak in order to be healed: "Who touched me?" and the disciples said: "Master, with all the people pressing you in on all sides, everyone's touching you!" "No, I felt power going out from me." The woman, who was caught off guard, prostrating herself, said: "It was I, Master."[33] This teaching is even clearer if one thinks back to the Canaanite woman: "Give a little bit of bread also to your other children." And He says: "No, I was sent for the sons of God, the Jews," and she replies: "Give at least the crumbs, you don't deny those even to the dogs." "Woman, your faith is great, I will heal you."[34]

To recognize that, in that church fifty yards from here, Christ is there, the man who lived and died and rose again in Palestine two thousand years ago; to recognize that He's there, in the bread, under the appearance of bread, in the sign of bread; to recognize this: I challenge you to find a greater sacrifice of oneself (of one's own intelligence, of one's own need to love, of one's own passion that the whole world know Him).

A few months after the birth of GS, a father, a very distinguished gentleman, whose daughter was at the Virgilio High School came to see me, and at the door he began to sob, saying: "Father, help me, save my daughter, because I can't go on any longer. When my daughter squeezes my hand," (his daughter was seventeen and was dying of cancer) "and tells me: 'Daddy, why don't you make me well?' it breaks my heart, because not only do I not know how to answer, but I don't even want to exist anymore." And I had to answer him: "The Lord knows why this is happening, and it's for your good and the good of your daughter, because this corresponds to God's plan." Thus I forced him to accept, to affirm the presence of Another who is more important, more decisive than the love for his daughter, than his desire to save her, more important than his very life..

To recognize the presence of another is always the beginning of a history of sacrifices – always. When a mother gives birth to a baby, it's the beginning of a history of sacrifices; when a boy marries a girl, it's the beginning of a history of sacrifices. But this is like the dawn of an ever more intensely laden day when man recognizes God made man as present, present in his life. You remember the comparison I made? If the President of the Republic went to our house on the Via Monte Rosa, first the whole house would prepare, clean, etc.; and when he came, everything would revolve around the President.

If God has become a man and is present to me and you, this Presence determines and defines, has the right to provoke and determine, my whole life, all of my relationships, everything that I do. It's here that the sense of disproportion emerges; but I'm sure that this disproportion, with His help, will be corrected, and this is the greatest joy that you can perceive in life: the certainty that my weakness will be won over by none other than Him whom my will and freedom should serve.

The greatest sacrifice is to recognize a Presence; this is something, the thing "from the other world." All of a person's experience is either summed up in this point of sacrifice, or everything falls apart. You can't pick it up again; you grasp it at one part and it slips away from another.

There's no greater source of sacrifice than a relationship with a person, to recognize a person. This holds true even for a mother's gaze upon her child, a man's gaze upon a woman, a friend's gaze upon a friend. For this reason, during the first days of school in my first year at Berchet, I used to say: "You've been together for five years, at the same table for five years and you're not friends – at most, you're accomplices."[35] For it not to become connivance but real friendship among us, it must first pass through Christ, you must first recognize that Christ is the most profound source of our life's pain, of our life's sacrifice: as He died, so must we die. And yet the human and existential reverberation of this sacrifice is joy, as He said: "I have told you these things so that my joy may be in you and your joy may be complete."[36]

3 Virginity

I will list the essential points around which the entire discussion of virginity revolves.

1 CALLED FOR A TASK

a) The choice of specific people
There is a premise, a premise that is no small thing: God became a man. You remember Monsignor Manfredini, my classmate, that night when we were going to church and we were late and we were running down the stairs – there are three or four flights of stairs. He was behind me, then suddenly he grabbed me by the arm and said: "Listen [we were twenty years old – no, not even], listen, to think that God became man is something belonging to the other world." This thing from the other world happened and divides the world. The first choice God makes is the choice of men who are called to understand this, so this choice is Baptism. But this is the antecedent.

Today's first point: To bring about His work in the world, Christ chooses some specific people. Imagine in the torchlight that night, before He died, imagine Him together with the twelve − if something is not yet part of your experience, you must try to make it an object of the imagination, you must try to imagine it, to become aware − He, and the twelve around the table who were silently watching that man speak, that man who said: "Without me you can do nothing," a man who sat down at the table with them, and said: "Without me you can do nothing."[1] "But this is …" they didn't say "He's God," but they felt that He was God. They didn't think it, they didn't understand it, but they felt it. To understand it, they had to wait for the Holy Spirit.

To complete His work, He chose some specific people … to whose names He added, in the course of time, our names, your names; if you're here, in some way He tugged on your hair; in some way, He at least brushed against your clothes; if you are here He touched you; in whatever way it happened, He touched you, He called you.[2]

b) To witness to Him

What did He call you for? To make his witness reverberate throughout the world, to make Him present in the world. On the seminary steps, at ten-thirty at night, that year, that time, Manfredini, in grabbing my arm, made Christ present to me. It was "something other" that grabbed my arm, it wasn't human logic, it wasn't a logic that was foreseen by my classmate. Who can say something like this? Certainly, if God was made man, it's something belonging to the other world; it's something from the other world that is here, among us now. And we must say it! In this toil or in this series of words there is "something else"; one wouldn't even be able to say this whole string of words if "something else" were not here. We are called to bear witness to Him.

c) *Living with Him*

How does one bear witness to Him? By living with Him. One who reads the gospel every day, one who goes to communion every day, one who says "Come, Lord," one who looks at certain companions on the path for whom this has already become more habitual, can begin to feel what it means to live with Him. Living with Him can be said in another way: living like Him.

d) *For the destiny of men*

How did He live? By conceiving of life – life is every action, even sleeping, even waking (at nine this morning, they came to wake me up), even eating, even drinking, and then all of living and dying – for the world, for God's plan in the world, that is, for all men and women. It is for men, for the people who are in Japan, for the people who are in Australia, for the people who are at the North Pole, for the people we don't know and whom we begin to perceive as part of ourselves, and so for whom one must give one's life. All that one does is for the life of men and women, for their destiny, so that they reach their destiny. We meditated on this when we spoke of charity: conceiving one's own life – you wake up at nine in the morning (however, I managed to fall asleep at five-thirty; I saw five-thirty and I fell asleep!) – for the destiny of others, which is something that begins to be not abstract because it has to do with the destiny of your father, of your mother, of the girl you feel affection for, of the boy you like, of the friends you have around you; it is the destiny of these people here. A man who looks at a woman whom he's in love with and whom he marries without ever thinking of her destiny is unbalanced; he makes both his and her lives *schizophrenic*; in fact they'll live in a schizophrenic way. And how many people are like this!

2 THROUGH SACRIFICE, THE HUNDREDFOLD

Sacrificing the immediate reaction

For me to be able to think of your life (you whom I don't know), to be able to think of your life as destiny, I must sacrifice something. To think of your life (you whose face I know), to love your destiny, to love your happiness, to love your contentedness, to love the eternity of your life, to treat you like this, I must sacrifice something. What must I sacrifice? I must sacrifice my immediate reaction, of liking or disliking, of sympathy or antipathy; I must sacrifice the immediate impression. The immediate impression upon seeing a beautiful woman … eh? I must sacrifice this. The immediate impression when thinking of a life "in a little house surrounded by trees." Pierre de Craon, standing in the midst of his cathedral as it was being built, directing all the work, thinks of a cottage with smoke coming out the chimney: my God, what a distance! God has called us to this distance, to live the world with this distance: the distance by which a cottage is a cottage and the temple the temple and the people the people (even the little woman who'd be his wife in that cottage belongs to these people).[3]

A sacrifice is needed, the sacrifice of what is immediate. The immediate is not true, so much so that it dies, it causes death. First it makes things old, it stifles the tongue, brings about rheumatism; one struggles to stay on one's feet. It makes things die, the immediate makes things die, the immediate dies in your hands. In the morning you're excited about your wife, in the evening you'd tell her where to go; telling her where to go means in the evening you'd kick her out: "If I could just be free of her!"

What is immediate binds, enchains, until one is strangled – in movies, when you see someone strangle someone, you see the other taking bizarre gasps and gurgles until … poof! The immediate strangles us. This strange phenomenon needs detachment. To truly love a person you need detachment: does a man adore his woman more when he looks at her from one metre away, in awe at the being he has before him, almost on his knees, even if he's standing, almost on his knees in front of her; or, when he takes her for himself? No! No, when he takes her for himself, it's over.

Who possessed Magdalene the prostitute more: Christ, who looked at her for an instant while she was passing in front of him, or all the men who had possessed her? When, a few days later, that woman washed his feet in tears, she answered this question.

You can't establish a relationship with anything – not with people, not with the flowers of the field, not with the stars in the sky – if not with an interior detachment. If you don't detach yourself from the stars, you don't understand: if you gazed at a star without detachment, you wouldn't understand that it is a star within the infinity of stars. It is sacrifice that allows the unveiling of the truth of the "thing" or "person" that is present.

A foretaste of eternal tenderness

Last point. This truth in the method of loving, which Christ possessed, astonished those who watched Him: they were awestruck. That man over there, who did not touch them – he touched the eyes of the blind, the mouths of the mute, he touched the ears of the deaf, to cure them, only that – when they arrived within twenty metres of Him, they were nevertheless pierced by that Presence inside Him, a Presence that remained with them for days, that required an effort to shake off! In this way, Christ put Himself in a relationship with people, bringing about a more useful love, a love that was more of a *company* on the path, a love that made the road lighter, a love that foreshadowed – like the skipping of a heartbeat – eternal tenderness, a love in all things that foreshadowed the relationship He had with John before dying, when John had His head on his shoulder.

This foretaste here in this world, this foretaste, in the relationship I have with you – even though I've seen you only once, this foretaste present in the relationship with you as I will see you forever in the clarity of the eternal, in the eternal transfiguration, in the seriousness of the eternal, is called the hundredfold here below. We are called every day, in the evening, to ask ourselves how much hundredfold we have lived. And it cannot be – as people say who come to me to complain – that they don't experience the hundredfold here below. What is certain is that you don't experience it because you imagine the hundredfold the way you want it, you imagine the hundredfold as the enlargement of instinct. Instead it's something else, it's something else that's more beautiful, that's more certain, that's more fascinating, that's more human, that makes you a brother or sister to the poor man who's reduced to almost a carcass, in the sewer at the edges of the street, who is about to die and whom Mother Teresa's sister takes, without being disgusted, and brings home. They give him a bath, they dress him ... and he, before dying, a few hours later, says: "I have always lived like a wretch and I'm dying like a king." Treated like a king, treated like a king: the hundredfold here below.

It may be that, word by word, sentence by sentence, you have understood everything. But what is missing is the experience of the connection of these words with your living flesh, what is missing is the life experience. May these words become the content of something felt, something lived, that sets you in motion, that moves you.

VIRGINITY: ASSEMBLY

Today, you must not only give your reflections on this morning's lesson, but on the whole year, on the situation that these words outline, point out: your difficulties, the objections you have, what you're not able to understand ... and I'll say: "It's impossible to understand!" But, dear friends, something else remains: what do you need to do?

He exists if He performs works; He changes, He changes you. You don't understand it, but He changes you.

The lessons on sacrifice and virginity were like cold water in the face for me, because of the deep contradiction that they contain, so I was wondering why there's this very mysterious contradiction that calls for a way that is so contrary to what it seems.

To allow the world to live – a hundred times more. You asked the most beautiful question possible. God, coming to this world, is something belonging to the world beyond, Jesus is something belonging to the world beyond. Take Jesus away: everything falls apart, meaning everything is razed, is burned – only ashes remain.

But with Jesus, nothing's lost any more – even your own evil remains, transformed into gratitude. And even your own evil, were it to be repeated a hundred times, the result of the hundredth time is to open you up to the hundred and first time, to open you up to the hope of overcoming it, because the overcoming of our evil happens when God wants it. You can't answer: "OK, so I'll do whatever I want; when God wants, He'll change me." No! You have to desire, to desire more. Look, a man can't look at a woman and say: "How beautiful!" and desire her, without desiring to be as perfect as she is beautiful. If he doesn't desire to be as perfect as she is beautiful, it's not true that he loves her. He'll abuse her and that's it.

One of the things that struck me this year was my work in the hospital. All of the nurses and even other doctors continually told me, "You are so different," and they asked me why.

You have to admit that this is the sign of the Mystery; the sign that there's a Mystery in this man, and that the others are forced to say: "You are so different." The Mystery is something different. One can't see, has no cure, goes into the water at Lourdes, sees: it's something different. There's nothing more consoling, more exciting, more astounding, more mysterious than the fact that others say: "Why are you so different? You are different."

And this is what really struck me, above all, because many people were saying: "We have to work with the other doctors, but with you, it's as if you were a friend."

This "You're different" is regarding his humanity, his whole person, not his surgical technique. Our own Enzo from Bologna is a fantastic surgeon, particularly in certain difficult operations, but no one says: "You're different" because of that. They say "You're different" because of the way he behaves. The difference is regarding the I, the man. The sisters of Mother Teresa couldn't heal that poor man, they couldn't heal him, but they were different. He himself said it: "You're different, and I'll die like a king." It's the humanity that's different, it's Christ's humanity that is different. When John and Andrew went together and watched Him speak that afternoon, in who knows what secluded hovel in the land of Judah, they said: "There's no one like this man." And the voice of the people: "He's a man, a man." To understand that there's a world beyond, you must have an experience of the world beyond, here in this world – not a dream, not an image (the world beyond), but an experience of the world beyond, here in this world.

More precisely, you must have the experience of the incompleteness of the things you do, which would be an impotent anger if it weren't for the hope and sweetness found in abandoning yourself.

Do you think that there's a more beautiful and greater work on earth than bringing this tenderness and certainty to the world? Answer me, answer me! A mother's work? A mother's work ... most of the time these days, they never look at their children, never even once, thinking of their children's destiny. Is that love? That's instinctive attachment. There may be the mother who's attentive to her child, who may never sleep, who's always vigilant to every sign: if she goes on like this, she'll die before long. But anyway, the child grows up, doesn't care about his mother, has other things, other things to do, that is, other things are more important to him. And the woman despairs, is bitter, and is capable of becoming unbelievably resentful.

Like that time in Milan when a thirty-year-old man came to me for confession: "I've been in a relationship with a girl for ten years." "After ten years – marry her!" "Well, but it's my mother." "What do you mean, your mother?" "My mother pays for any prostitute that I want, she brings them home, provided that I don't get married, in order not to lose her son – and she's a woman who does an hour of Eucharistic adoration every day." For her, Jesus would have been the clang of a cymbal, at best, if she had had imagination and musical taste. But it's highly improbable that she had any, because a person with musical taste can't help but realize the dissonance of her attitude. And, in fact, with Jesus, either you end up singing or the relationship ends! With Jesus, it's impossible not to end up singing, even for one who is tone-deaf; even when the uvula gets messed up, you sing with the heart!

You said that the truth in a relationship coincides with maintaining the attractiveness of the relationship. Lately I've understood that for me, when the aspect of renunciation prevails in my relationship with things or work, it's as if there was something that wasn't right, something wrong, because you said that the truth in a relationship maintains all the zest of that relationship.
Not in the same way.

I want to know why, then, there's the temptation to think that the two things aren't united.
Because you think about a relationship with an inflection that you don't want to give up (who among us hasn't experienced this?) and that you need to give up – and it's a dramatic moment – in order to possess. Because esteem and love are maintained only if you detach yourself from your immediate and usual way of feeling about things. If you want to go on according to the immediate and usual way you feel about things, you'll lose them. It's not my fault – that's the way it is! Even from a natural standpoint it's like that. If you want to climb to the top of Monte Rosa, you have to leave the valley behind, that beautiful valley! You keep your gaze on the valley's beauty with a different inflection that keeps *everything* in mind, that makes it different. You don't leave it behind, you climb the mountain. In going toward destiny, you don't leave anything behind,

you draw everything with you toward destiny: "You have ravished me with only one of your hairs," the Song of Songs would say;[4] "Even the hairs of your head are counted.[5] I want to remind you of the story of Giovanni Guareschi that appeared in the magazine *Il Candido* after the war. It concerned a man and a woman, both in their eighties, seated on the balcony outside their home, watching people take their afternoon stroll. He: "How beautiful your hair is" – she had three strands of hair! "How beautiful your hair is." In saying that, he said something with a truth, a poetry, a lasting value, that he didn't have at the time he fell in love with her and she had a full head of blond hair. He was young, he was constricted before.

Faithfulness that is kept, keeps everything, but keeping faithfulness is a sacrifice. A man falls in love. While out with his wife, he sees a certain woman on the other side of the street. He looks the other way;[6] he has to give up something, he has to tear himself away. And the faithfulness to his wife will be rewarded – not right away, but in the course of time. Yet over the same time, if he had followed that other woman, she would have disappeared, thirty-four years before!

I'd like to say something that really struck me about this year's path regarding the question of vocation. I'm a good friend of a woman who's dying of cancer, who wrote: "Without you, I wouldn't have known the loving face of the Mystery that makes all things." This really struck me, precisely with respect to vocation, because if I think about my vocation during this period, I can't help but think of her and what she's living. And if

I think about her, I can't help but think that she's living
something of a vocation. I realized that a person like her thought
of her life in a certain way, she raised a family, but at a certain
point, something happened, which forces one either to answer
to a vocation which the Lord calls her …

Either you're placed in front of something with virginity, because virginity is life as vocation.

… or else, you're left only with desperation. It became clear
to me when you said that there's no alternative between Christ
and nothingness. We can think about our lives in whatever way,
but we can fulfill our lives only if we pass through this answer
to life as vocation, only by answering affirmatively to this calling.

Virginity is to profess the presence of God in the world; Christ, this man, here and now. Apart from this, there's nothing, everything ends up in nothing. The letters of Mounier to his wife[7] are pages of virginity, where the ideal of marriage is virginity – so much so that you speak of matrimonial chastity, right? So then, man's vocation is virginity, essentially. And to this virginity, God gives either one task or another. There is only one vocation. If He gives a certain task, that of the family, it's then that Saint Peter says, after considering everything, "If that's the case, it's better not to get married."[8]

One can be on this path, having walked down it all year, yet
the hypothesis of a different path – the cloister, for example –
can persist or arise. I wanted to ask what this idea means.

Do you give yourself the vocation? We need to distinguish the recognition of a vocation – and this is an objective fact – from the affirmation of one's own image, of one's own imagination. The first characteristic of an affirmation of one's own image is that it's always wavering. The second characteristic is that it doesn't come about all of a sudden, clearly, but rather as something in opposition. You are here, there's no other idea, no other fact that is clearer and simpler than this, this given fact: you are called. Where are your schoolmates? Your schoolmates – where are they? They're not here; why aren't they here? Flo had lots of friends at the Università Cattolica [the Catholic University in Milan]. Where are they? They're at the Università Cattolica! This is a given fact: the relationship with Christ is always a given fact – a fact. It can be accompanied right away by a big halo of light, of feeling, of tenderness, of strength, of faithfulness, of sacrifice; sacrifice becomes like a poem, it takes on the rhythm of poetry, of a song. But the first word, the most fundamental word, the cornerstone of the foundation is a given fact: if you are here, in some way you were touched by something. I'm sorry, it's not my fault! I would be at fault if I didn't do anything to keep you here. That's why we say the Hail Mary to the Blessed Mother for our Portuguese doctor who works in England.

Just as the vocation was given to you, it is preserved for you in front of the world by the same thing, that is, by the same hand, by the same face of Christ that told you "Come," and said "Come" to people who are like all the others.

Last night, we read about Violaine, who was fully ready to follow the hand that led her.[9] *This is really what I desire, but it also scares me. What should I do?*

Eliminate the fear, as much as you're able to. If you're not able to, follow the hand anyway. To follow the hand with fear has the same effect as following the hand without fear; the essence of the question is to follow the hand. By following the hand, you say: "Listen, let me be less frightened, let me be less frightened, let me be less frightened." After the fifteenth time, you discover that you're no longer afraid. Afraid? Of what? Of nothingness; but the nothingness isn't nothingness, it's a lie.

Do you realize that in everyone who tells a woman "I love you," there's at least one aspect that's a lie? Yet, in saying "Lord, I love you," it's more difficult to lie, because one who says that has an easier time understanding all his mistakes. When Saint Peter answered Jesus – who had asked him "Simon, do you love me"? – "Yes, Lord, you know that I love you,"[10] think of how he had in mind all the mistakes that he had made!

One time, you told us that the human I is the crossroads between the relationship with the Eternal and nothingness, which is abstraction. What I ask for most is that these words become the substance of my life.

In Rimini, I said that the I is the crossroads between the eternal and nothing, and existentially and historically this becomes real, as either the recognition of Christ or not.[11] The "no" said to Christ, not saying "Christ," is the same as saying "Everything is nothing." Tell me logically how this can end up differently – tell me! This is so true that the highest human ideal, which seems to be the Buddhist one, conceives of the solution to everything as a drop that falls into the ocean, and mixes into the ocean, the harmonious ocean of everything. What beautiful harmony! Where the I disappears! Disappearance is what you're aiming towards.

You told us last Saturday: what appears abstract is what has already been eliminated in terms of judgment of pertinence.
Yes, what seems abstract is something that we've already said no to. Because if I didn't say no, even if it appears abstract, then I understand that I have to go through all the struggles necessary to make it concrete, to make it an experience. Everything we've said to you, I swear to you will become experience. It's become experience for us – that's why we're here. We'd have to have a lot of courage to gather so many people together like this in order to tell a lie. You can't have courage to do something like this – you'd need to be a politician or maybe a panderer: it's always a question of money, because power is only about money.

Something is either true or not true; to say that something true is abstract means that you've already said no: what appears abstract is what we've already denied. If they tell you something that appears abstract, you must commit yourself to see how you can concretize it, and in this attempt to make it an experience, you learn it. Do you understand?

It's like the difference between a threat and a promise.
To tell you something abstract that isn't true is a threat, it's holding you under the terror of a threat. Most of the clergy don't realize that they're doing this: they hold the people under a threat. Most of the clergy, parents, or politicians,

everyone: he who doesn't love your person and doesn't love his destiny holds you under a threat.

On the other hand, what seems abstract to you is a promise, not a threat – not a threat that lessens the relationship with the boy or girl you love. It's a promise that you'll have more.

It's beautiful to see these things from the vantage point of seventy years of life, like me … the buzz of the people that you've run into since you were fifteen. The way that you ran into them comes to mind, the desires that sprang up, the mistakes made, the mistakes made, the mistakes made … all this buzz and seeing again the faces that you don't ever forget. And you understand, without realizing it, that you're saying: "O Father, may we all be joined together" – you pray for them, understanding what you understand is essential – "may they also reach their destiny." Then, you find them again, you find them in a way that's a hundred times better than it was when you were twenty.

So, there are so many questions to ask that we could remain here together until next June. Our whole life is a questioning, *quaestio*, the quest for an answer. What's the most important condition in searching for an answer? Not having preconceptions. When one is on this path and continues to entertain the doubt that maybe there's another path (and this is certainly not asking for a change!), one makes a fundamental error, in that the image establishes a preconception about the data of reality. This reality has all the reasons on its side – all of them! I challenge you to give me one reason to the contrary – go ahead, I dare you! Ever since I began teaching religion in school forty years ago, I've never heard one objection that I hadn't already had myself and that I hadn't already answered. Because I might be a fool, but only up to a certain point – that is, Christ's fool. In the seminary, we formed a small group with Manfredini, Biffi, called Christ's Fools, after a saying used by a common nineteenth-century Russian devotion. Anyway, this is a witness that I must make: I've never had a question, even at school, a question that I hadn't already asked myself and that I hadn't answered. If they had asked me a question on *De magnetite*, I wouldn't have known it. It's about things that aren't true that I wouldn't know the answer. OK, next!

This morning, it was said that Christ chose us to stay with Him, and it seems as if I am living the same experience as the first disciples who said: "It's beautiful to be here, let's not go to the people." But then, what does the world have to do with anything; where is the "for the world"?
Very true, and in fact, we shouldn't remain here; we have to go out to all the world. Our friends, only counting those from Italy, are in twenty-six countries, missionaries. So get in line to go on the mission.

You said that when something that is told you seems abstract, it's because we've already rejected it. I'd like to know the reason.
If I tell you something that seems abstract to you, you should look for the reasons, not say: "It's abstract." To say "It's abstract" is to affirm a feeling, not a reason. Have I made myself clear? If we tell you something that seems

abstract to you, you should look for its reasons from us, with us. Reasons are what link a statement to life; reason ties things to life, to reality. Seek the reasons; but this involves work, continuous work, patience, reflection, a half hour of silence daily. It involves studying the School of Community, it involves studying our texts, it implies work: finding reasons implies work. On the other hand, to say that something we say is abstract without this work of seeking the reasons, means affirming a feeling, a mood – it's a purely sentimental reaction. Christ is present. Where is He present? Here, here and now.

Christ is present here.

Sentimental reaction: "But no, but no!" This is the process of abstraction.

But if I tell you that He's here, and you ask: "Why do you say He's here? In what sense is He here? How is He here?" then I'll give you a series of reasons and reason allows you to better discover reality, not the feeling of abstraction or non-abstraction.

Isn't having an objection like "It's abstract" also denying something evident?
Evidence is given by the reasons that one perceives, the reasons that one understands, that one follows intuitively. Evidence is nothing more than the result of the heart's mechanism that is called reason – evidence is the result of reason. Reason is the crossroads of what is true, the mine of the truth. To say that the things we say are abstract is to affirm one's own imagination, to privilege a psychological reaction, not a reason.

For example, when at school, I used to say: "You have an objection, do you have some opposing reasons? Tell me them!" Silence. "So then, why don't you come with me?" This is the fraud in man: the betrayal of what is true. The whole crowd that followed Jesus seven days before wanted to make Him king because He had fed them for free. Seven days later they were yelling: "Crucify Him!" following the suggestion of the Pharisees. It's irrational, it's without reason.

Either Christ or nothing. If Christ isn't true, there is nothing, everything falls into nothing. It's the Buddhist image of reality, a pantheistic one, in which everything flows back and dissolves: that is beauty. No, it's an ugly fantasy; it doesn't explain anything, except for restating the vanity of everything. Without Christ, everything is vain; without a Presence, there's the void.

All these things we've said always well up in me a greater desire, but I wonder: "How can I respond to Christ more, in order to become more of a man?"

Listen, follow us! He placed you with us, good God! God placed you with us. It's not our fault that He put you with us; we're all stuck here, we in the first place. And Carlo, who didn't want to care about anything, who wanted to do his own thing, is forced to be here, is forced! I, on the other hand, thank God, I was always happy, because it's true. Carlo, tell us your first impression in religion class.

I thought that it wasn't possible to use reason like this. It wasn't that I made a conscious comparison with my use of reason before,

*it was that this use of reason made me understand that until
then, I hadn't ever used it, and I hadn't ever seen it used.
And then, I remember that the first thing that I said is:
"If this guy here believes, I have to believe, too, I have to take
it seriously, too." From infancy, I had the impression that
everyone spoke nonsense and I didn't think that there could be
another way.*

He was already bad when he was young. The intelligence
of a young boy who has the impression that everyone
speaks nonsense, empty words, is amazing. For a young boy
to have this impression ... he'd truly be an intelligent kid.

*It often seems to me that the things I hear and the things that my
friends testify to aren't yet part of my experience, and this hinders
me. You told us to take a look, in the evening, during the day,
and to ask ourselves how much we lived the hundredfold.
My tendency is to measure, but it seems that the question is not
one of measure. Instead, you pointed out the position of the
apostles in front of Christ as the true position. I want to ask
how to be in this position of the apostles.*

The position of the apostles – imagine what it was like.
Let's imagine that Jesus is here, and we're all listening to
Him. We don't understand what He says, but I'm paying
attention, because He says it in such a way that you understand that He sees, that He knows, that He hears, that He
lives this. So I'm paying attention to Him because I also
want to grasp something; I understand some pieces of sentences, some shreds of words, and in the end, I ask: "Jesus,
make me understand what you said." The apostles did this
with the parables. With the parables, they didn't understand

what they meant; in the end, they pressed Him and said, "Master, explain what this parable means."

So, at night, don't measure, but ask: "Thy kingdom come, Thy will be done," "Come, Lord Jesus," which is the cry that ends the Bible.[12] The whole Bible ends with this cry, and shouldn't my day end with this cry? One who does this every night is alive (not like us oftentimes), he's a changed man. If you do this every night, you're changed, and you have to do it with strength but without any claims, because you don't know when the Son of Man will come into your life, when He'll take you by the collar and will change you, force you to change, or He'll charm you irresistibly in order to change you.

If not for this deeper gaze, this fascinating hope, what do you live for? You may even find a girl who is beautiful in your eyes – to make the comparison that the Lord forced us to make by creating Adam and Eve: He had compassion on Adam because it wasn't good for him to be alone and he gave him Eve as a companion – and then? And then? And then? Then, I wish that you live a hundred years, and then? Without this "And then?" humanity doesn't exist, you give up your brain, you abolish reason, your heart dries up. Whoever doesn't have this hope has a dried-up heart. It's because of this that European man, whose whole history is Christian, treats Bosnia as he treated it, treats Rwanda as he treats it, as he treated Vietnam, as he treated Korea: with hatred, with violence. His weapons destroyed everything possible. Without Christ, you destroy.

A truth about life must also bring with it life's wounds. You can't respond to life by imagining it without wounds when it's full of wounds. Whereas, a word or a way of looking at life that embraces life even with all of its wounds is true. For this reason, a woman, a mother of three, who is dying of cancer, writes: "Without you and without the movement, I never would have known the good face of the Mystery that makes all things." It would have been desperation, but instead, she's not desperate. Like that mother of my friend, whose son unexpectedly died and she writes a letter full of mistakes, because she's almost illiterate. At a certain point, she makes a point and says, without any logic: "But I'm happy, because God is great."

Virginity is the profession in the world that brings this to the world, that doesn't make peace with fraud, with evil, even though we have fraud inside us, we have evil inside us. Therefore, the first result is that we change: He exists, if He performs works; He exists, if He changes; He exists, if He changes.

Therefore, the answer to give our English friend is again that of reason: in front of the uncertainty and the disagreements, seek the reasons: "You tell me that Christ is here; what reasons do you give?" And pay attention to my reasons and don't say no to the reasons that you don't understand yet; say: "I don't understand," and I'll tell you: "Ask to understand, beg to understand." And this is right for man, because man, who is nothing, was made as a thirst for being, that is, a beggar for being, a beggar for life, a thirst for life.

What does the promise of the hundredfold here below have to do with the fact that, in my more lucid moments, there's a veil of sadness surrounding me?

The veil of sadness is given by what? This is rational investigation. Is the veil of sadness given by the promise of the hundredfold or is it given by some deficiency that you tolerate? If you, for example, don't beg, if you don't follow Him, if in your life, you don't follow Christ, if in your life you don't follow us, if we don't join together, we don't search together, how can you have the hundredfold? Where does this veil of sadness come from? It's because you remain attached to having, to possessing immediately, as you feel, instead of desiring to feel the way you should, to feel what is true, carrying your cross like Christ, like all men. "When I was born" – when I was ten, I studied a poem that began like this – "When I was born a voice told me: you were born to carry your cross"[13] (now, they don't make you study these poems anymore, but it was a very beautiful poem). Here the word "cross" isn't the *finis rei*, it's not the end of the story; the story doesn't end with the cross, it begins with it: the cross is a condition. "You want to climb Monte Rosa: you have to take this road here, with these passes." "I'm afraid." "If you give in to your fear, you'll never climb Monte Rosa!"

My friend, follow us. Since we have the same flesh, the same heart – we're men – what we've done you can also do, right? Listen, what we've done is a hundred times better than what we see everyone else do – so much so that, in the end, they come running back to us.

The very first time I walked into school, first period, I walked into class and went to the teacher's desk. "Oh God, I haven't even spoken yet and someone's already got an objection!" His name was Pavesi. He wrote me for his wedding, saying that for twenty years the name that was always on his lips was the name of the religion teacher. At his wedding, I told him, "In what you didn't follow me until today, follow me now, because you'll have children; therefore, let's save them from the sorrows that you didn't save yourselves from."

Lately, it has happened several times that I was almost forced, strongly, to compare what was happening to me with the things I heard you say. I realized that to accept everything for Christ isn't enough if there's not something of a safe place where you can experience this, and I was wondering if there's this safe place for me.

Your question isn't one that I share, because sacrifice, to be accepted, requires us to have a secure point, but not secure in front of the sacrifice! You can't be sure of the sacrifice – you're sure of Christ, not of the sacrifice. If you're sure of Christ, the question is simple; if you believe, you'll have the hundredfold.

Faced with sacrifices, your only resource is to perceive your sacrifice as part of Christ who climbs up on the cross, who dies for the world; your sacrifice counts for all men's pain, it alleviates all men's pain: maybe there's a person suffering in Japan and, at the end of the world, she'll say "Thank you," because your sacrifice in that moment helped her. No gesture exists that does not involve the whole world. That's why we get up every morning: to help Christ save the world, with the strength we have, with the light we possess, asking Christ to give us more light and more strength.

This morning, a beautiful prayer was read: "so that in loving You in all things and above all things,"[14] in loving this man, Christ, in all things and above all things. "In all things" is clear (in all things: even a strand of hair on your head) and "above all things" – as is said in *Un avvenimento di vita, cioè una storia*[15] – doesn't mean that Christ is above; "above" means within every visible aspect of the question, more inside everything that we can see, more inside every visible thing, more inside, deeper than any reason and visible substance. The prophecy of this lies in the love that a mother has for a child and a man has for a woman – when they are true. When they are true, there's a foretaste of this, but they wouldn't know how to express it. Humanly speaking, reason wouldn't know how to express it. Only when Christ came did men understand.

What struck me most this year was the wonder at becoming aware of how much the Lord really cares about my life, and this was understood both throughout the day and when we got together with the group leaders. In this way, it became easier at the end of the day to say "You" to Christ. A little while ago, maybe I would tell friends "Let's say a prayer to the Lord"; now, instead, at night, it's easier to say, "Lord, thank you for having placed me close to these friends."
At night, it became easier for you to say "You," to say "You." Who can we better say "you" to than this "You"? It's only because of this "You" that also the "you" that we say to the person we love, to all the others, takes on substance; it also personalizes our relationship with everyone.

Let's pray to the Blessed Mother that she watch over us during this vacation period: that vanity not win out over reason, that appearance not win out over what is true, that the nameless does not win out over the only indisputable, clear, overriding name – which is that of Christ. We're all nameless. If there were no Christ, we'd all be nameless: everything would be merely a breath.

Notes

CHAPTER 1

1 From the Sunday morning hymn, "The morn dawns refulgent with glory." In *Book of Hours*. Milan: Coop. Edit Nuovo Mondo 1992, 25.

2 "Yes, you speak truly Girolama; I am not as I was.
  I see better, and nevertheless I was not blind;
  But it was the light, doubtless which caused the imperfection;
  For the light from without is a poor thing;
  It is not that which illumines our life.
  You have lit a lamp in my heart:
  And lo! I am as a sick man who falls asleep in the shadows,
  With the dew of fever on his brow and the chill of destitution in
      his heart, and then awakes with a start in a beautiful chamber
  Where all things bathe in the shining music of light;
  And lo! The friend whom he wept for long years gone.
  The friend returned from the ocean lands is there"
  Who smiles upon him with eyes more calm, more wise than of yore,
  And all the family is there, old men with snowy heads
  And children clad in the light of harvests, and the fat old dog

Is there, his large eyes drowned in tender laughter

And his mouth wide open and full of barks of joy

To make carnival for the man saved from the deluge of darkness!

See what a place of peace you have made in my heart, Girolama.

And thanks, and great thanks, to you, Girolama!"

O.V. Milosz, *Miguel Mañara: A Mystery in Six Scenes*. Edward J. O'Brien, trans. In *Poet Lore* (summer 1919), 236–7.

3 L. Giussani, "The Journeying." In *He Is If He Changes*. Rome: 30 Days, 1994. 12–16.

4 1 John 4:16.

5 John 15:5.

6 Giussani is referring to an annual gathering of university students in Communion and Liberation that takes place at the Charterhouse of Pavia on Holy Thursday. During the morning there are readings of chapters 14 to 17 of Saint John's Gospel.

7 Genesis 1:26.

8 John 15:13.

9 Romans 5:20.

10 *See* Luigi Giussani, *At the Origin of the Christian Claim*. Viviane Hewitt, trans. Montreal and Kingston: McGill-Queen's University Press, 1998. 80–98.

11 "This day of our Easter rejoicing,/Our innocence He will renew." From the Sunday morning hymn, "The morn dawns refulgent with glory." In *Book of Hours*. Milan: Coop. Edit Nuovo Mondo, 1992. 25.

12 Luke 13:34–5.

13 Luke 19:41–4.

14 Luke 7:11–17.

15 Luke 19:1–10.

16 John 11:1–44.

17 Psalm 8:5.

18 The weekly magazine (no longer in print), *Il Sabato,* and the monthly
   30 Days had numerous articles, beginning in 1991, on the problem
   of the historicity of the gospels and the apostolicity of the Roman
   tradition.

19 *See* John Paul I's *Angelus* of 10 September 1978, in *Avvenire*,
   29 September 1978, special insert, 4.

20 "Very deep is the well of the past. Should we not call it bottomless?
   Bottomless indeed, if – and perhaps only if – the past we mean is
   the past merely of the life of mankind, that riddling essence of which
   our own normally unsatisfied and quite abnormally wretched exis-
   tences form a part." Thomas Mann, *Joseph and His Brothers.* H.T.
   Lowe-Porter trans. New York: Alfred A. Knopf, 1968. 3.

21 Matthew 5:48.

22 Luke 6:36.

23 John Paul II, *Redemptor Hominis* (1979), chapter 9.

24 Jan Palach was a Czech student who committed suicide in January
   1969 in Wenceslas Square in Prague, by setting himself on fire. He
   was protesting the Soviet-led invasion of Czechoslovakia a few
   weeks earlier, and thus became a symbol of resistance.

25 Translated from Charles Péguy, *Le mystère des saints innocents.* Paris:
   Gallimard, 1929. 72–3. Part of the translation is adapted from Pansy
   Pakenham's abridged version of *The Mystery of the Holy Innocents and
   Other Poems.* London: Harvill Press, 1956. 106–7.

26 See Isaiah 50:7.

27 1 John 4:11.

28 See Matthew 5:48 and Luke 6:36.

29 1 John 4:16.

30 See Luke 10:25–7.

31 See Giussani, *At the Origin of the Christian Claim.* 92–5.

32 Galatians 2:20.

33 Don't conform yourselves!" In Greek: "me suskematizesthe." The
   word contains the root of the word "scheme." Briefly: every exterior

model, every scheme is empty! We must reach for much more. The Apostle calls us: "Transform yourselves in the renewal of your mind." With the plasticity of his expressions, Paul tells us: one doesn't change according to some model (which always ends up out of style anyway), but by introducing into us the richness of a substantial newness. J. Zverina, "Lettera aperta ai cristiani d'Occidente" (Open Letter to the Christians of the West) in *Litterae Communionis* 9, September 1992: 3.

34 "Anniversary: I can read between your lines" G. Clericetti, *Clericettario*. Milan: Gribaudi, 1993. 30. Editor's note: In the original Italian there is a play on the Italian words *righe* (lines) and *rughe* (wrinkles). The literal translation is "I can read between the wrinkles."

35 O. Mazzoni, *Noi peccatori: liriche 1883–1936*. Bologna: Zanichelli, 1930. 72.

36 See Philippians 1:6.

37 Giovanni Pascoli, "Il cieco," in *Poesie*. Milan: Garzanti, 1974. 277–81.

38 Giussani, *The Religious Sense*. John Zucchi, trans. Montreal and Kingston: McGill-Queen's University Press, 1997. 105.

39 Alain Finkielkraut, "Péguy: la forza dell'evento," in *30 Giorni* 11 (November 1992): 52–5.

40 Giussani, *Why the Church?* Viviane Hewitt, trans. Montreal and Kingston: McGill-Queen's University Press, 2001. 123ff.

41 Paradiso, Canto XXXIV, 89–91.

42 Tomás Luis De Victoria, "Caligaverunt oculi mei," in "Responsories from Holy Week." Giussani would have this hymn sung during his meditations on Holy Thursday and Good Friday.

43 John 17:1.

44 See Song of Songs 4:9.

45 1 Corinthians 13:1–13.

46 Giussani, *Il tempo si fa breve: Esercizi della Fraternità*, supplement to *Litterae communionis – Tracce* 7 (1994): 9.

47 Dionysius The Areopagite, *On Divine Names*, XI: v. "What would any one say of the peaceful stream of love towards man in Christ."

CHAPTER 2

1 In Italy, thirteen is a lucky number.

2 Cesare Pavese, *Il mestiere del vivere.* Turin: Einaudi, 1973. 191.

3 See Luigi Giussani, *The Religious Sense*. John Zucchi, trans. Montreal and Kingston: McGill-Queen's University Press, 1997. 137–8.

4 See Psalm 115: 4–8.

5 Famous Italian soccer players.

6 Giussani, *Un avvenimento di vita cioè una storia* (*An event of life, that is, a history*). Rome: EDIT Il Sabato, 1993.

7 John 15:13.

8 Rev. 22:20.

9 There sighs, complaints, and ululations loud/Resounded through the air without a star, Whence I, at the beginning, wept thereat. *Inferno*, canto III, 22–24 (Longfellow translation).

10 *See* John Paul II, *Address to the Youth of Rome,* 24 March, 1994. Supplement to 30 *Giorni*, (4), April 1994.

11 John 14:12.

12 *See* John 14:12; John 15:5–16.

13 *See* Giussani, *He Is if He Changes*. Supplement to *30 Days*, February 1994.

14 Jacopone da Todi, "O novo canto." "A Canticle of the Nativity." In *The Lauds*. Serge and Elizabeth Hughes, trans. Ramsey N.J: Paulist Press, 1982. 195.

15 Giussani, *Il tempo si fa breve: Esercizi della Fraternità*. Supplement to *Litterae communionis – Tracce 7 (1994): 9.*

16 Giussani, *The Religious Sense*, 74.

17 Eugenio Montale, "Perhaps Some Morning…" In *Provisional Conclusions*. Edith Farnsworth, trans. Chicago: Henry Regnery Co., 1970. 40.

18 Psalm 118:107.

19 See Wisdom 1:13–15.

20 1 Corinthians 3:11.

21 Matthew 10:8.

22 Concluding prayer from Saturday midday prayer, in *Book of Hours*. Milan: Coop. Edit Nuovo Mondo, 1992. 200.

23 "If you believe in god and no god exists,/ then your belief is an even greater wonder./ Then it is really something inconceivably great./ Why should a being lie down there in the darkness crying to someone who does not exist?/ Why should that be?/ There is no one who hears when someone cries in the darkness. But why does that cry exist?" Pär Lagerkvist. In *Eveningland aftonland*. W.H. Auden and Leif Sjöberg, trans. Detroit: Wayne State University Press, 1975. 127.

24 Giussani, "Un inizio e una storia di grazia." In *Un avvenimento di vita*. 453.

25 John 14:31.

26 John 5:17.

27 John 5:30.

28 Philippians 2:8.

29 John 16:32.

30 John 17:1.

31 See Matthew 26:42; Mark 14:36; Luke 22:42.

32 Luke 12:49.

33 See Matthew 9:20–21; Mark 5:25–27; Luke 8:43–44.

34 See Matthew 15:21–28; Mark 7:24–30.

35 See "La comunione come strada." In *Litterae Communionis: Tracce* 7 (July-August 1994), insert, v.

36 John 15:11.

CHAPTER 3

1 John 15:5.

2 See Mark 3:13–18.

3 In Claudel's work, Pierre de Craon is the architect, the genius whose artistic expression and way of life bring people to rediscover their unity, which is to say they rediscover their dwelling place. This dwelling place contains both the ideal and every failing. And all the people find themselves equal in front of the infinity of the ideal and in front of the misery of their errors. So the architect-builder of cathedrals is the genius par excellence, because the cathedral constitutes the greatest symbol of unity among men that was ever thought of. Pierre de Craon – as intense and passionate as he was ingenious – in the face of the vocation given him by God has something like a moment of hesitation: "After so many sublime steeple tops, shall I never see the top of my own small house among the trees? So many spires whose shadow as it turns inscribes the hour over every city! Am I never to make the drawing of an oven or of a children's room? an oven or a bedroom for the children?" Paul Claudel, *The Tidings Brought to Mary*. Wallace Fowlie, trans. Chicago: Henry Regnery Company, 1960. Prologue, 19.

4 See Wisdom 4:9.

5 Luke 12:7.

6 Luigi Giussani, *The Religious Sense*. John Zucchi, trans. Montreal and Kingston: McGill Queen's University Press, 1997. 29–30.

7 Emmanuel Mounier, *Mounier et Sa Génération: Lettres, Carnets et Inédits*. Paris: Seuil, 1961.

8 Matthew 19:10.

9 "That is how Violaine immediately follows the hand which takes hers." Paul Claudel, *The Tidings Brought to Mary*. Wallace Fowlie, trans. Chicago: Henry Regnery Company 1960. Act IV, sc. 2, 127.

10 John 21:15

11 Giussani, *Il tempo si fa breve: Esercizi della Fraternità*. Supplement to *Litterae communionis – Tracce 7 (1994)*.

12 Revelations 22:20.

13 "When I was born, a voice told me:/ you were born to carry your cross / and I crying embraced the cross / that from heaven was assigned to me. / Then I looked, looked, looked / everyone carried the cross here below. / I saw a king among barons and men with shields / under the weight of dark thoughts and I asked the valet: / "What is your king thinking about down here?" / And he answered: "The cross that he is carrying / that the Lord with the throne gave him." G. Panzanese, in *Per la scuola per la vita,* a book of readings at that time for the first year of high school.

14 Prayer from the twentieth Sunday in Ordinary Time in the Ambrosian Liturgy.

15 Giussani, *"Qui salvandos salvas gratis."* In *Un avvenimento di vita cioè una storia* (An event of life, that is, a history). Rome: EDIT Il Sabato, 1993. 303.

Index to volumes 1, 2, and 3 of
Is It Possible to Live This Way?

86, in Christ, 7, Christian, 94,
continuity of, 72, dynamic of,
17, 18, in Jesus, 7, 48, in Jesus
Christ, 12, lack of, 28,
obedience of, 108, reason by,
20; III: 4, 22, 43, 47, 63, 67, 68,
82, 100, sacrifice of, 82

for Christ, 24, for destiny, 67,
for money, 22, for reason, 66;
III: 6–12, 15, 18, 20–4, 26–33,
35–9, 43, 44, 48–53, 59, 61–3,
67–9, 72, 74, 78–84, 87, 89,
91–3, 97, 98, 100, 106–8, 110,
112–14, 117, 119, 128, for
Christ, 66, 76, for destiny, 38,
106, 119, eternal, 12, 18,
law of, 33
loyalty, I: 21, 123; III: 77

mediation, I: 3, 9, 10, of a trusted
person, 7, of a witness, 8, 9
method(s), I: 8–10, 13, 14, 20–2,
25, 79, 110, of faith, 11, 14,
21, 22, of knowing, 20, 21,
of knowledge, 8, 20, 21, of
reason, 21, 27; III: 74, 95, of
loving, 108
morality, I: 24, Christian, 77; II:
47, 81, 118, origin of, 117; III:
11, 20, 22, 27
mortification, I: 72, 73, 78, 81;
III: 85
mystery, I: 11, 13, 15, 19, 50,
65–7, 69, 72, 73, 78, 83, 85, 94,
95, 97–100, 107, 128, 139, 146,
155; II: 23, 24, 36, 38, 42, 45,
48, 69, 108, 123, 124, 127–30,
132, 136, 143, 153; III: 4, 8, 16,
17, 19, 28, 42, 46, 47, 57, 62,

83, 87, 89, 94, 95, 98, 99, 111,
114, 125

nature, I: 31, 112, 113, divine, 138,
of our heart, 39, of our "I",
39; II: 41, 52, 53, 55, 95, man's,
53, phenomenon of, 95; III: 8,
12, 19, 55, 56, 68, 76, 78, 91,
97, God's, 8–10, 19, 26, man's,
75, of man's destiny, 86, 89,
meaning of, 78, reality of, 29
nothingness, I: 38; III: 12, 16, 18,
62, 85, 115, 117

obedience, I: 102, 103, 116, 118,
126, 128, 130, 131, 134–40,
142, 144, 153, 155, 156, attitude
of, 128, to Christ, 128, to the
Father, 101, 102, 128, to God's
plan, 20, of heart, 155, law of,
158, unity of, 156; II: 86, 87,
107, of faith 108, to God, 48;
III: 44, 48

passion, I: 17, 52, 158; II: 49; III:
16, 65, 100
penitence, I: 72, 73
perfection, I: 63, 65, 95; II: 15, 16,
23, 117, 118; III: 20
personality, I: 12; II: 3, 7, 71,
72, 103
philosophy(ies), I: 52, Saint

Thomas's, 66, scholastic, 24;
II: 33, 43, of life, 43,
modern, 129; III: 23, human,
26, modern, 49

possession, I: 12, 105–7, 114, of
being, 107, of God, 106; II:
14, 24, 56, 57, 67, 87–9, 93,
95, 111, 143, of Christ, 88,
of God, 143, of things, 110;
III: 98, 107, 113, 126, 127, of
Another, 32

prayer, I: 15, 17, 18, 34, 55, 78, 79,
119, 127, daytime, 17, 18, 20,
117, to God, 15, 25; II: 14, 44,
45, 124, to God, 76, mid–day,
121; III: 23, 29, 44, 87, 119,
128, 129, morning, 3

preconception(s), I: 39–41, 59,
60, 68; III: 24, 119

reality, I: 7, 10, 11, 13, 14, 16,
18, 19, 28, 29, 39, 44, 51, 95,
105–8, 114, 122, 152, 153, ad-
hering to, 105, 106, 155, affirmation of, 106, awareness of,
152, of Being, 98, Christian,
148, consciousness of, 109, of
creation, 99, 105, God's, 19,
knowledge of, 7, 9, 153, of
the Mystery, 98, order of, 18,
path to, 114, understanding
of, 148; II: 11, 32, 62, 75, 78,

105, 106, 109, 122, consciousness of, 11, 32, experiential,
104, intelligence, 104, matrimonial, 122, of a people, 142,
of a person, 142, present, 31,
relationship with, 98, weight
of, 83; III: 3, 25, 27, 36, 49, 56,
57, 90, 119, 121, awareness of,
4, 48, beauty of, 28, of being
moved, 14, Buddhist image
of, 122, concreteness of, 49,
of nature, 29, pagan, 15,
of the Spirit, 28, supreme, 4, 5

reason, I: 3, 7–14, 18, 20, 22, 25,
27, 29, 39, 40, 42, 52, 55, 105,
109, 113, 122, 126, 134, 152,
153, act of, 105, 134, capacity,
14, evidence of, 24, fruit of,
57, 's knowledge, 130, locus
of, 42, man's, 129, method(s)
of, 20, 21, 27, opposite of, 114,
use of, 22; II: 4–8, 12, 18, 21,
36, 41, 45, 47, 48, 61, 82, 87,
90, 91, 93, 121–5, 128, 129, for
action, 59, distraction from,
91, for living, 46, unity in, 41;
III: 4–8, 12, 18, 21, 36, 41, 47,
48, 82, 90, 91, 121–5, 128, 129,
unity in, 41

reasonableness (unreasonableness),
I: 3, 6, 7, 9, 13, 22–4, 48, 52,
55, 59, 71, 84–6, 97, 103, 116,

Name index

Beethoven, I: 96; II: 134, 135

Biffi, Giacomo, III: 120

Bloch, Ernst, II: 137

Bobbio, Norberto, II: 76

Camus, Albert, II: 76, 153

Carracci, Annibale, II: 144

Cesbron, Gilbert, II: 151

Chopin, Frédéric, II: 134, 135

Clericetti, Guido, I: 87; III: 40

Colombo, Giovanni, II: 101

Columbus, Christopher, II: 14

Dante (Alighieri), I: 63, 65; II: 26, 56, 98, 126; III: 53

de Craon, Pierre, III: 106

De Foucauld, Charles, II: 152

Delafosse, Maurice, II: 43, 44

De Victoria, T.L., III: 54

Dionysius, III: 63

Fra Angelico, III: 30

Galbiati, Enrico Rodolfo, II: 116

Giotto di Bondone, II: 140

Guareschi, Giovanni, III: 114

Hegel, G.W.F., II: 58

Homer, II: 86

Ibsen, Henrik, II: 72

Kafka, Franz, II: 76

Lagerkvist, Pär, I: 147; II: 46, 108; III: 89

Lazarus, I: 40; II: 47; III: 14

Lievers, Strik, III: 21

Luther, Martin, II: 50

Manfredini, Enrico, I: 41, 42,
    130, 131, 148, 150, 151;
    II: 8; III: 103, 104, 120

Mann, Thomas, II: 79; III: 19

Mauriac, François, II: 91, 92

Melchizedek, II: 46

Moeller, Charles, I: 81

Mondadori, Arnoldo, III: 21

Montale, Eugenio, II: 80; III: 85

Mother Teresa, III: 22, 25, 60,
    109, 111

Mozart, Wolfgang Amadeus,
    I: 96

Palch, Jan, III: 61

Pascoli, Giovanni, I: 42; II: 6;
    III: 43

Pasteur, Louis, I: 59

Pavese, Cesare, III: 68, 93

Péguy, Charles, I: 39, 100, 113;
    II: 12, 36, 51, 55; III: 23, 47

Pope John Paul I, III: 17

Prophet Jeremiah, III: 12

Ratzinger, Joseph (now Pope
    Benedict XVI), I: 155; II: 83

Rebora, Clemente, II: 80

Rizzoli, Angelo, III: 21

Saint Andrew, I: 28, 29, 32, 33,
    43, 44, 48, 49, 53, 54, 57, 58,
    73, 76, 82, 154, 155; II: 10, 14,
    28, 29, 54, 105, 111–15, 144,
    146, 148, 153; III: 4, 11, 15, 81,
    82, 111

Saint Augustine, II: 53

Saint Clare, II: 102

Saint Dominic, III: 30

Saint Francis Borgia, III: 40

Saint Francis of Assisi, II: 91,
    95, 102

Saint Gregory the Great, II: 9

Saint Iranaeus, II: 10

Saint John the Apostle, I: 28, 29,
    32, 33, 43, 44, 48, 49, 53, 54,
    57, 58, 73, 76, 82, 154, 155;
    II: 14, 28, 29, 54, 105, 111–14,
    144, 146, 148, 153; III: 4, 11, 81,
    82, 108, 111

Saint John the Baptist, I: 26, 58

Saint John the Evangelist, I: 27,
    32, 34, 38, 40, 43, 68, 73, 77,
    127–9, 138; II: 14, 28, 31, 34, 54,
    105, 113, 117, 118, 144, 148, 149;
    III: 4, 8, 13, 14, 20, 21, 26, 81

Saint Joseph, II: 47

Saint Luke, III: 13, 20

Saint Mark, II: 15; III: 13

Saint Mary Magdalen, II: 84;
    III: 107

Saint Matthew, I: 35, 55, 142;
  II: 47; III: 13
Saint Maximilian Kolbe,
  I: 101; III: 39
Saint Nathanael, I: 43, 44
Saint Paul, I: 71, 93, 99, 103,
  127–9, 137; II: 7, 31, 37, 45, 67,
  80, 84, 92, 93, 110, 116; III: 21,
  24, 29, 34, 41, 61
Saint Philip, I: 33, 34; III: 14, 15
Saint Polycarp, II: 10
Saint Thomas Aquinas, I: 50, 66,
  77; II: 27

Saint Thomas apostle, III: 84
Salvaneschi, Nino, II: 102
Schweitzer, Albert, II: 151, 152;
  III: 18
Seneca, I: 69; III: 27, 30
Socrates, I: 69, 78

Virgil, II: 76
Von Speyr, Adrienne, II: 79

Wagner, Richard, II: 76

Zaccheus, II: 29; III: 13, 14